D1601553

Constructing Peace

Constructing Peace

Lessons from UN Peacebuilding Operations in El Salvador and Cambodia

Lisa A. Hall MacLeod

LEXINGTON BOOKS

A division of
ROWMAN & LITTLEFIELD PUBLISHERS, INC.
Lanham • Boulder • New York • Toronto • Oxford

LEXINGTON BOOKS

A division of Rowman & Littlefield Publishers, Inc.
A wholly owned subsidiary of The Rowman & Littlefield Publishing Group, Inc.
4501 Forbes Boulevard, Suite 200
Lanham, MD 20706

PO Box 317
Oxford
OX2 9RU, UK

British Library Cataloguing in Publication Information Available

Library of Congress Cataloging-in-Publication Data

MacLeod, Lisa A. Hall.
  Constructing peace : lessons from UN peacebuilding operations in
El Salvador and Cambodia / Lisa A. Hall MacLeod.
    p. cm.
  Includes bibliographical references and index.
  ISBN-13: 978-0-7391-1096-6 (cloth : alk. paper)
  ISBN-10: 0-7391-1096-9 (cloth : alk. paper)
  1. Peace-building--El Salvador. 2. Peace-building--Cambodia.
3. United Nations--El Salvador. 4. United Nations--Cambodia.
I. Title.
JZ5584.S2M33 2006
959.604'3--dc22   2005035379

Printed in the United States of America

℗™ The paper used in this publication meets the minimum requirements of American
National Standard for Information Sciences—Permanence of Paper for Printed Library
Materials, ANSI/NISO Z39.48–1992.

Contents

Chapter 1

UN Peacebuilding and Civil Conflict

The end of the Cold War created great optimism that the United Nations would finally be allowed to realize its intended purpose to "save succeeding generations from the scourge of war." Since that time, the United Nations has developed new strategies to facilitate the resolution and transformation of both international and civil conflict.[1] The now prominent role of United Nations peacekeepers in the resolution of civil conflict was not anticipated by the authors of the UN Charter. Peacekeeping was developed during the Cold War as an operational response to the UN's mandate to protect *international* peace and security. The primary role of traditional peacekeepers was to monitor cease-fire agreements. They were deployed with the consent of the disputing parties and authorized to use force only in self-defense. The immediate goal of traditional peacekeeping was not in itself to end armed conflict. Rather, peacekeeping was viewed as a "conflict containment" strategy. It was hoped that freezing the situation on the battlefield would facilitate diplomatic peacemaking on a separate track.[2] With few exceptions, the dynamics of Cold War politics and prevailing interpretations of the principle of nonintervention enshrined in Article 2(7) of the UN Charter prevented active UN involvement in the resolution of civil conflict. These factors, however, did not prevent the United Nations from deploying peacekeepers to states experiencing civil war and other forms of political violence. Five of the thirteen peacekeeping operations created during the Cold War are best understood as responses to civil conflict in Lebanon, Congo (Zaire), Yemen, Cyprus, and the Dominican Republic (James 1992a).

During the Cold War, UN peacekeepers deployed to countries experiencing civil conflict were primarily concerned with preventing superpower escalation and foreign support of insurgents. Peacekeepers were deployed to ensure the

UN Peace Operations, 1945-1979

UN Mission	Date	Location	Type of Conflict
UNTSO	1948-	Israel-Egypt-Syria-Jordan-Lebanon	International Conflict
UNMOGIP	1949-	India-Pakistan	International Conflict
UNEF I	1956-1967	Israel-Egypt	International Conflict
UNSF	1962-1963	Netherlands-Indonesia	International Conflict
UNIPOM	1965-1966	India-Pakistan	International Conflict
UNEF II	1973-1979	Israel-Egypt	International Conflict
UNDOF	1974-	Israel-Syria	International Conflict
UNIFIL	1978-	Lebanon-Israel	International Conflict
UNOGIL	1958	Lebanon	Civil Conflict
ONUC	1960-1964	Congo	Civil Conflict
UNYOM	1963-1964	Yemen	Civil Conflict
UNFICYP	1964-	Cyprus	Civil Conflict
DOMREP	1965-1966	Dominican Republic	Civil Conflict

conflict was both *contained* within national borders and that it was *de-internationalized*. In most cases, the primary function of peacekeeping was to monitor and verify the withdrawal of foreign forces and support. Unlike UN responses since the end of the Cold War, these operations did not seek to mediate a negotiated settlement between the internal parties to the conflict and focused instead on preventing domestic insurgents from receiving external assistance. What contact UN peacekeepers had with non-state actors was usually limited to the provision of humanitarian relief to non-combatants and *ad hoc* arrangements to monitor international borders in rebel-controlled areas.[3]

The spirit of cooperation of the immediate post-Cold War period resulted in the creation of a number of new UN peace operations. Only five (UNMEE, Ethiopia/Eritrea, 2000-present; UNIKOM, Iraq/Kuwait, 1991-2003; UNASOG, Chad/Libya, 1994; UNIIMOG, Iran/Iraq, 1988-1991) were established to monitor cease-fire agreements between sovereign states. The overwhelming majority of UN peace operations created since 1989 were responses to armed political violence within states.[4] Many of these operations included mission mandates beyond the parameters of traditional peacekeeping to include peace enforcement, humanitarian intervention, and post-conflict peacebuilding operations. Of the innovations of this period, post-conflict peacebuilding — operations mandated to aid implementation of negotiated settlements to civil conflict — marked a significant new role for the United Nations. The organization founded on the principle of non-intervention in the domestic affairs of member states came to play a prominent role in the resolution of civil conflict.

Through peacebuilding, the United Nations not only became involved in the negotiation and implementation of settlements to end civil conflict; the United Nations became an advocate of a particular model of domestic political legitimacy. The adoption of peacebuilding coincided with and was likely the result of the international community's embrace of what Linz and Stepan labeled the "democratic *zeitgeist*" of the post-Cold War era (1996, 74). In the decade following the collapse of the Berlin Wall, the democratic peace hypothesis was expanded into the domestic realm.

> Democracy ... was said to be a foundation of 'peace and security.' That 'democratic' states don't go to war with one another' became a cliché for many member states and UN officials, and Boutros-Ghali himself stated that democratic states were more legitimate than others and were less likely to have domestic conflicts or become embroiled in regional wars. (Barnett 1999, 190)[5]

Peacebuilding sought to address the underlying causes of civil conflict and create "the political conditions for sustainable, democratic peace" (Bertram 1995, 388).

The UN's first full-fledged experiment with peacebuilding took place in 1989.[6] Peacekeepers were dispatched to Namibia where they monitored the withdrawal of foreign fighters, supervised the disarmament and demobilization of internal combatants and observed human rights, as well as supervised the

UN Peacebuilding Operations, 1989-2005

UN Mission	Date	Location	Peace Settlement
UNTAG	1989-1990	Namibia	Geneva Protocol
ONUSAL	1991-1995	El Salvador	Chapultepec Accords
UNAVEM II UNAVEM III MONUA	1991-1995 1995-1997 1997-1999	Angola	Lusaka Protocol
UNAMIC UNTAC	1991-1992 1992-1993	Cambodia	Paris Peace Accords
ONUMOZ	1992-1994	Mozambique	General Peace Agreement (Rome)
UNOMIL	1993-1997	Liberia	Cotonou Peace Agreement
UNAMIR	1993-1996	Rwanda	Arusha Peace Agreement
UNMOT	1994-2000	Tajikistan	1997 General Peace Agreement
UNMIBH	1995-2002	Bosnia and Herzegovina	Dayton Accords
UNTAES	1996-1998	Croatia	Basic Agreement
MINUGUA	1997	Guatemala	Oslo Agreement
MINURCA	1998-2000	Central African Republic	Bangui Agreements
UNAMSIL	1999-	Sierra Leone	Lomé Peace Accord
MINUCI UNOCI	2003-2004 2004-	Côte d'Ivoire	Lina-Marcoussis Agreement

country's first democratic election. Three additional peacebuilding operations —
in Angola (UNAVEM II, 1991-1995), El Salvador (ONUSAL, 1991-1995), and
Cambodia (UNAMIC/UNTAC, 1991-1993) — began in 1991. A fourth peacebuilding operation began in Mozambique (ONUMOZ, 1992-1994) the following
year. These missions shared many characteristics, including the deployment of
military and civilian peacekeepers following formal agreement by the domestic
parties to the conflict, supervision of demobilization of forces, and UN technical
and other support for democratization and related reforms. As of January 2005,
there were twenty completed and ongoing UN peacebuilding operations in sixteen countries. Additionally, several missions containing peacebuilding elements
such as electoral assistance, human rights monitoring, and civilian police training have been deployed where armed conflict ended as the result of international
intervention including operations in Kosovo, East Timor and Afghanistan.

Despite the initial optimism of the early post-Cold War period, durable
transformation of civil conflict remains an elusive goal. The UN's experience
with peacebuilding is mixed. Peacebuilding operations in Mozambique and El
Salvador led to the creation of democratic institutions that have endured long
after the departure of blue helmets. To date, return to armed political violence
has been avoided. Outcomes of other operations have been less successful. In
Cambodia, only three of the four domestic signatories of the Paris Accords participated in UN-sponsored elections. Electoral results were all too soon over-
turned by political intimidation and violence. Elections in Angola were quickly
followed by the outbreak of renewed fighting as bloody as any period in the
country's violent history.

Demand for better understanding of the causes of success and failure of
post-Cold War UN peace operations triggered an explosion of new publications,
primarily in the form of descriptive histories[7] and typologies.[8] Analyses of
peacebuilding operations have drawn from studies of third-party mediation and
conflict resolution,[9] democratization,[10] and the relatively new field of civil war
termination.[11] Unfortunately, most studies of UN peace operations are published
during or shortly after the operation's formal end making it difficult to differen-
tiate between peace processes that lead to a short-term suspension of fighting
and more durable conflict transformation. The question remains "What forms of
third-party assistance are most likely to support a sustained transformation of
civil conflict?" Licklider's study of civil war termination indicates that negotiated settlements that do endure for five years seldom collapse in future violence
(2001, 698). This finding suggests that settlements that endure for at least five
years following the withdrawal of international forces can be described as durable conflict resolution or what Cousens labels a "self-enforcing peace" (2001,
11). The studies of UN peacebuilding operations in El Salvador and Cambodia
that follow are, therefore, primarily concerned with identifying those variables
that contributed to the durable transformation of conflict in El Salvador and
were missing or lacking in the Cambodian case.

Ending Civil War

Efforts to bring an end to civil conflict pose special challenges to would-be peacemakers. Historically, violent civil conflict has been more likely to end with the military victory of one side and the defeat of the other. This however, is an undesirable outcome as civil wars that end in this manner are "often associated with widespread human rights abuses, atrocities, genocide, environmental degradation and a host of other ills" (King 1997, 12). Negotiated resolution to civil conflict is, therefore, the preferred option. Between 1940 and 1990 only 20 percent of civil wars ended as a result of a negotiated settlement (Walter 1997). The likelihood that a negotiated peace agreement will be reached and implemented is enhanced when third-parties support the peace process (Walter 1997, 2002).

Third-parties have played a significant role during both the negotiation and implementation phases of peace process designed to end civil war.[12] Third-parties often play a crucial role in aiding the peace process by helping participants recognize that the conflict is "ripe for resolution." The ripe moment is widely understood as the point in which both sides are "unable to escalate the conflict with their available means and at an acceptable cost" (i.e. a mutually hurting stalemate) (Zartman 1995, 8). Ripeness is often as much a matter of perception than objective reality. Through granting or denying aid, third-parties can shape conditions on the battlefield to bring about a mutually hurting stalemate. Third-parties can also influence the perception of ripeness. Once the parties to the conflict come to accept that negotiations promise a preferred outcome to continued stalemate, third-parties can support the peace process through the provision of good offices and mediation (Zartman 1995).[13] Third-party efforts to resolve civil war are more likely to succeed when powerful external actors and neighboring states support the peace process. Past mediation efforts on behalf of the UN Secretary-General have benefited from the support of interested states.[14]

Negotiation of a formal agreement is but the first step in the peace process. Negotiated settlements are notoriously difficult to implement. As Chester Crocker observed,

> Just as conflicts seldom resolve themselves, peaceful settlements do not implement themselves. The role of foreign interveners cannot end on the day that agreements are signed. Implementation mechanisms are essential to keep things on track, to sustain the political chemistry that produced the deal, and to continue linkages and pressures that led to the breakthrough. As in other fields of endeavor (law or business), statecraft illustrates the maxim that the real negotiation only begins after the agreements are signed. Outsiders who orphan the settlement they have helped produce will watch them collapse.
>
> (1996, 194)[15]

Every peace process has challengers and would-be spoilers. Not all benefit from peace. Ripeness needs to be "cultivated" throughout the peace process (Hampson 1996a). This may involve creative interpretation or outright re-negotiation of agreements during the implementation process, monitoring and verifying compliance, and mobilizing resources to enable implementation and punish noncompliance.[16] Third-parties that extend credible security guarantees can help the parties overcome fears that implementation of the terms of the peace accords, particularly disarmament and demobilization provisions, will lead to vulnerability should the peace process collapse (Walter 1997, 1999; King 1997).

UN peacebuilding operations are mandated to monitor and assist the critical implementation phase of peace processes. In theory, peacebuilding helps participants in civil war to overcome the inherent challenges of implementing negotiated settlements. The outcome of these operations has varied greatly. Most analysis focuses on the perceived failings of UN peacebuilding operations including accusations that the international community failed to provide adequate resources to support implementation; the often unstated corollary being that sustainable peace would have materialized had not the international community is tried buy peace on the cheap in Angola and other cases.[17] The unique geographic and social environments to which peacebuilding operations deploy make direct comparison of budgets inappropriate. Comparison of resource allocation (reflected in the cost of each mission) by population and/or geography gives a better sense of the actual operational capacity of each mission relative to the environment in which it operated. Comparison of total operational costs and cost as a function of population and territory reveal no obvious correlations with respect to durable conflict resolution. If operational success is a direct function of the amount of resources spent on peacebuilding operations, one would expect to see the greatest success in Cambodia. Instead, many aspects of that operation's mandate (including disarmament of the factions) were not fully implemented, not all parties to the peace accords participated in UN-sponsored elections, and political backsliding led to a coup in 1997. If cost/territory is the relevant measure, then operations in El Salvador should have met with less (not more) success than the Cambodian mission. If cost/population is the most relevant measure, the Salvadoran operation should have had a similar outcome to that in Angola. Instead, peacebuilding operations in El Salvador, Namibia, and Mozambique have all experienced durable conflict transformation. There are no direct correlations between cost, however measured, and the outcome of peacebuilding operations.

There is an additional problem with this mode of explanation. Resource-oriented studies of peacebuilding explain the actions of the parties in terms of cost-benefit analysis. While in the short-term it is not difficult to match compliance or non-compliance with positive and negative inducements of third-parties, this is an inadequate account of long-term conflict transformation. Once peacekeepers depart, why do some conflicts resume while others do not?

Lack of resources is but one account given for the perceived failings of UN peacebuilding operations. Another popular explanation of peacebuilding failures is the argument that some peace agreements were doomed to failure because they called for the creation of conflict-prone institutional forms. Although the

UN Peacebuilding Operations Facts and Figures					
Peacebuilding Operation	Cost ($ mil.)	Population (mil.)	Total Area (sq. km)	Cost / Pop.	Cost / Area
UNAMIC/ UNTAC	1,621.0	12.8	181,040	127	8,954
ONUSAL	107.0	6.5	21,040	16	5,086
ONUMOZ	492.6	19.6	801,590	25	615
UNTAG	368.6	1.8	825,418	205	447
UNAVEM II	175.8	10.6	1,246,700	17	141

UN Secretariat and many member states have come to embrace democratization as an important peace strategy, there is little consensus as to which institutional forms best facilitate the conflict transformation and the creation of a durable peace. The rhetoric employed by many member states and UN officials assumes only a very general definition of democracy: free and fair elections, respect for the civil and political rights of individuals, and the rule of law (Joyner 1999, 334). Policymakers and scholars continue to debate the merits of parliamentary versus presidential institutional structures and winner-take-all versus proportional voting systems. Parliamentary democracy is viewed by some as the system most likely to protect minority rights and foster political compromise thus ensuring the stability of the post-conflict settlement by ensuring the capacity of previously warring parties to protect their key interests. Similarly, proportional representation is advocated because it is believed to provide greater opportunity for all groups to participate in the division of political spoils. In contrast, a presidential institutional structure and winner-take-all voting system are deemed more likely to exclude some groups from power. Divested of a stake in the new government, it is feared that former combatants will have little incentive to cooperate in the post-election peace process.[18]

Examination of actual peacebuilding operations, however, suggests no direct correlation between institutional design and the durability of democratic transitions. The winner-take-all system in Angola is cited as a primary motive for UNITA's post-election return to violence.[19] In the case of Cambodia, where the terms of settlement included a system of proportional representation, election results were never reflected in the relative distribution of actual power in post-conflict political institutions. In contrast, the UN supported peace process in El Salvador, maintained the presidential institutional structure and winner-take-all electoral system of El Salvador's 1983 constitution. The lack of a direct correlation between institutional design, electoral system and the durability of democratic transitions suggests these variables alone are insufficient to explain the durability of conflict transformation.

Constructing Democratic Political Norms

The creation of a durable peace in the aftermath of violent civil conflict is a difficult task. While material and diplomatic resources are needed to cultivate peace throughout the transition process, peace is not created by simply throwing resources at the problem. Likewise, the resolution of violent civil conflict by means of a democratic transition requires much more than free and fair elections. The successful implementation of a negotiated settlement involving a democratic transition also requires the creation of a "democratic cultural norm of political action" (Peceny 1999, 97-98). The literature on civil war termination has identified political norms or legitimacy as an important factor in the initiation, resolution and prevention of armed conflict. Holsti, for example, identifies legitimacy (which he defines as "shared principles of justice") as a "pre-requisite" for peace and durable peace settlements (Holsti cited in Hampson 1996a, 20).[20] Similarly, Cousens identifies the creation of "political processes and institutions that can manage group conflict without violence but with authority and eventually, legitimacy" as the "most effective means to self-enforcing peace" (2001, 12). Legitimacy — understood as the shared "assessment" of the "degree of congruence, or lack of it, between a given system of power and the beliefs, values and expectations that provide its justification" (Beetham 1991, 11)[21] — is presumed to be an important component in the ability of political leaders to implement policy, maintain the loyalty of their followers, and avoid revolt against their leadership during the negotiation phase of a peace process. The capacity to implement negotiated settlements has also been linked to legitimacy, making it a factor in the outcome of peace operations.[22] The durable resolution of violent civil conflict, therefore, may depend on the successful negotiation and implementation of new norms of political legitimacy. Understanding the processes by which such norms take hold can be expected to provide policy relevant insight as to how third-parties can better support the creation of a durable peace during the negotiation and implementation phases of a peace process.

Originally developed to explain the mechanism by which human rights norms spread and come to be adopted by sovereign states, Finnemore and Sikkink's three-phase model of the social construction of *self-sustaining* norms suggests one process by which third-parties can support the development of new

---

Finnemore and Sikkink's Model of Norm Construction

	Norm Construction Phase	Key Indicators
Phase 1	Articulation of New Norms	Norms as articulated in statements, speeches, and agreements.
Phase 2	Strategic Social Construction	Compliance with new norms in sequence with material incentives and/or disincentives.
Phase 3	Self-sustaining New Norms	Political action is justified in terms of the new norms after aid conditionality is withdrawn.

---

norms of political legitimacy (1998).[23] In the first phase of the Finnemore and Sikkink model, norm entrepreneurs articulate and justify new norms. In the case of peacebuilding, norms are expected to be communicated in the formal terms of the peace, public reports, and public statements by parties involved in the conflict (usually the leadership of the conflicting parties and third-party mediators). In the second phase, strategic social construction, norm entrepreneurs engage employ diplomatic and financial incentives and disincentives to gain compliance with the norms articulated in the first phase. The allocation of financial resources, technical assistance, and other forms of aid by peacebuilders and other third-party supporters of the peace process can enable and reward compliance and punish noncompliance when aid is conditioned on the successful negotiation and implementation of the terms of peace.[24] In the third phase of norm construction, compliance with new norms becomes self-sustaining as short-term calculations of interest result in long-term systemic change. As Peceny notes, "Over time, the 'practice' of politics under new rules becomes embedded in the actors as norms for appropriate behavior, which in turn reinforces the norms." (1999, 97-98) Third-party supporters can aid peacebuilding by supporting the construction of democratic norms that de-legitimize political violence and legitimize non-violent conflict management mechanisms.[25]

The structured, focused comparison of UN peacebuilding operations in El Salvador (ONUSAL, 1991-1995) and Cambodia (UNAMIC/UNTAC, 1991-1993) that follow examine the relationship between the processes of social construction of democratic norms of political legitimacy and the durable settlement of civil conflict. Because peacebuilding operations in El Salvador and Cambodia took place at roughly the same time, it is assumed that many external factors such as relations between the great powers and the international balance of power are constant for both cases. Both cases took place amidst the "democratic *zeitgeist*" (Linz and Stepan 1996, 74) of the post-Cold War period and benefited from international mediation influenced by this spirit. The two peace processes also benefited from the support of interested and resource-rich states. There are, however, significant differences in how outside actors supported the construction of democratic norms of political legitimacy during the negotiation and implementation phases of the peace process. Though initially heralded as a partial success following the repatriation of thousands of refugees and relatively peaceful elections, UNTAC is considered a failure by the criteria used in this study. The coup of July 1997 and political violence during and after the peacekeeping operation bear witness to the fact that UN peacebuilding operations did not lead to the creation of a self-sustaining democratic transition as envisioned in the Paris Peace Accords.[26] While no peacebuilding operation runs exactly as planned, El Salvador has been able to avoid a relapse of political violence and has experienced enhanced democratic participation as a result of the implementation of the Chapultepec Accords. Though the implementation process had its challenges the Salvadoran case is considered a qualified success; there has been no large-scale return to political violence more than five years following the withdrawal of UN forces. Whether or not third-parties proved willing to support UN peacebuilding operations with strategic social construction of democratic and human rights norms provides a compelling account of the different outcome of these cases.

Notes

1. While *conflict transformation* and *conflict resolution* are often used interchangeably, Rupesinghe argues that this confuses the goal of peacemaking. Because conflict is a normal and sometime beneficial feature of human relations, the appropriate goal of peacemaking is not the resolution or end of conflict but rather conflict transformation such that the relationship between the parties is transformed "from one expressed through violence and arms to one expressed through non-violent means" (1998, 3). Also see Hampson (1996a), Kumar (1998), Lund (1996), Burton (1990), and Lederach (1997).

2. For example, in reference to the 1958 UN Observation Group in Lebanon (UNOGIL), Brian Urquhart described "the main objective [to keep] the cold war out of the Middle East" (1972, 265). For other references to early peacekeeping as conflict containment, also see Miller (1967, 65), Durch (1996), Goulding (1993), and Urquhart (1987, 128).

3. Exceptions did exist. Peacekeepers in the Congo (Zaire) aided the defeat of the Katanga succession movement, used military force in defense of the mission and provided limited protection to refugees. Peacekeepers in Cyprus assisted refugee relocation

(what came to be called ethnic cleansing in the context of the former Yugoslavia). See Higgins (1981; 1969).

4. This number can be misleading as it includes multiple missions created in response to the same conflict. For example, UN operations created in whole or in part as a response to the civil war in Angola include: UNAVEM I, UNAVEM II, UNAVEM III, and MONUA. Even with this taken into consideration, UN responses to civil conflict in the post-Cold War period far outweigh those created to address conflict between sovereign states.

5. Also see Joyner (1999, 350).

6. The United Nations Good Offices Mission in Afghanistan and Pakistan (UNGO-MAP, 1988-1991) was the first UN peace operation mandated to seek resolution of an on-going civil conflict (Birgisson 1993).

7. See The United Nations (1990; 1996), Diehl (1994), Durch (1993; 1996), Hill and Malik (1996), and Ratner (1995).

8. See Bratt (1997), Hill and Malik (1996), James (1990; 1993), MacKinlay and Chopra (1992), Pirnie (1994), Weiss (1994,), and Jablonsky (1999).

9. See Zartman (1985; 1996), Touval (1985), and Bercovitch (1996).

10. See Dahl (1989), Diamond (1996), Diamond et al. (1997), Farer (1996), Forsythe (1996), Huntington (1991), Linz and Stepan (1989; 1996).

11. See Walter (2002; 1997; 1999), Hampson (1996a), Stedman (1990; 2001), King (1997), and Licklider, et al. (1993).

12. See Cousens (2001), Licklider (1993), King (1997), and Walter (2002; 1999).

13. Also see Zartman and Touval (1996) and Hampson (1996a, 1996c).

14. See de Soto's account of the 'Friends Mechanism' in the Salvadoran peace process (1999). Also see Hampson (1996a; 1996b; 1996c), Doyle, Johnstone and Orr (1997), Munck and Kumar (1998), Fortna (1995), Jett (1999), Ohlson and Stedman (1994), Zartman and Touval (1996) and Durch (1993).

15. Also see Hampson (1996a; 1996c) and Kagan (1995).

16. See Hampson (1996a; 1996c), Doyle, Johnstone and Orr (1997), Munck and Kumar (1998), Fortna (1995), Jett (1999), Walter (1997; 1999; 2002), and Boyce (2003).

17. See Fortna (1995), Anstee (1995; 1996) and Parsons (1995).

18. See Hampson (1996a; 1996c), Doyle, Johnstone and Orr (1997), Walter (1999), Diamond (1996), Munck and Kumar (1998), Fortna (1995), and Jett (1999). Ottaway, however, cautions against putting too much emphasis on institutional structures warning that under certain conditions proportional representation can take on the feel of a winner-take-all system "if one party wins an overwhelming victory" (1998, 148). This argument is also made in the literature on democracy in (ethnically) divided societies. See Horowitz (1985) and Neuberger (1986).

19. See Fortna (1995), Anstee (1995; 1996), MacQueen (1998), and Knudsen and Zartman (1995).

20. Also see David (1997), Kumar (2001), Zartman (1997; 1993; 1995; 1985), James (1992b), Bar-Simon-Tov (1994), Rothschild (1981), Durch and Schear (1996), Ohlson and Stedman (1994), Kellas (1991), Horowitz (1985), Nordlinger (1972), Hansen (1997), and Rupesinghe (1998).

21. "Legitimacy is established by showing that the decisions accomplish appropriate objectives or by showing that they are made in appropriate ways." (March and Olsen 1989, 49) The construction of political legitimacy can be viewed as creating a 'domestic' regime "constituted by convergent expectations, shared principles and norms" (Ruggie 1998a, 85).

22. See Zartman (1997; 1993; 1995), James (1992b), Bar-Simon-Tov (1994), Roths-child (1981), Durch and Schear (1996), Ohlson and Stedman (1994), Kellas (1991), Horowitz (1985), Nordlinger (1972) and Rupesinghe (1998). See Fishel (1998), Stedman (2001), Adibe (1998, 113) and Hansen (1997). Hansen specifically notes, "... the elements of political legitimacy are assessed with respect to whether they can fulfill the population's needs for effectiveness, stability and security. These factors will determine the success of confidence-building measures and thus lasting peace." (1997, 75) Also see Wagner (1993) on this point.

23. Wendt's 'Three Degrees of Internalization' describes a similar process by which coercive, material and ideational forces combine to socially construct new intersubjective norms of legitimacy (1999).

24. James Boyce is the leading proponent of "peace conditionality." In the short term, peace conditionality seeks to ensure the implementation of negotiated settlements and in the long-term the "consolidation" of peace (Boyce 2002).

25. This process is similar to Ruggie's concept of "norm-governed change" by which norms become habitual because the behavioral changes initiated by external incentives have created new social structures thereby influencing actors' interests (if not the actors themselves) and relative cost and benefits their actions (1983; 1998). Also see Hurd who notes, "most social structures first emerge from relations of coercion or from individual self-interest; but once established they may come to develop supporting and independent bases of legitimacy" (1999, 389). Also see Snyder "[I]ntervention can provide the capability to monitor and enforce new institutional arrangements during a transitional period until locals' expectations converge on the new pattern and vested interests in the new status quo emerge" (1999, 27).

26. Most analyses of UN peace operations in Cambodia were published prior to the 1997 coup. See Doyle (1995; 1994; 1995), Hampson (1996a), Heininger (1994), Jeldres (1993), Munck (1995), Johnstone (1997), Ratner (1993b; 1993a), Sanderson (1994), and Schear (1996).

Chapter 2

El Salvador

In January 1992, the Salvadoran Government and the *Frente Farabundo Martí para la Liberación Nacional* (FMLN) signed the Chapultepec Accords, bringing an end to twelve years of armed conflict that resulted in the loss of some 75,000 lives. With the assistance of the United Nations Observer Mission in El Salvador (ONUSAL), a self-sustaining peace was created. The relationship between the former combatants has been transformed from bitter enmity and mutual suspicion to competitive partnership in a shared political framework. Since the departure of blue helmets, former antagonists participate in democratic institutions that provide the widest representation of society in any Salvadoran government since independence. Political violence is no longer recognized as a legitimate or normal course of action.[1]

The successful transformation of Salvadoran political life is all the more remarkable given the bitter and bloody history of the conflict. El Salvador slid into civil war in the late 1970s amid extreme economic inequality and the effective political exclusion of most Salvadorans. Political life was monopolized by a coalition of wealthy landowners and military leaders held together by a shared interest in the *status quo* and the willingness to use force to secure it. Groups seeking social and economic reform turned to armed resistance when their demands were met with violent repression. They joined forces under the banner of the FMLN in late 1980 (Lungo Uclés 1990). As the war against the FMLN became associated with preventing the spread of Communism in the Americas, the Salvadoran government and military became recipients of large amounts of American aid. The Salvadoran government, backed by the Reagan administration, demanded complete demobilization and disarmament of the FMLN as a precondition of political reform. The FMLN refused and called for formal power sharing in a transitional government. With no mechanism to guarantee its security, the FMLN was reluctant to disarm prior to negotiating a political settlement. The violence continued as the FMLN refused to surrender and the Salvadoran Government proved unable to defeat its enemy.

In 1989 a number of factors sustaining the armed conflict began to change. El Salvador's once unified economic elite split into two groups, each with distinct economic and, therefore, political interests. The first group maintained its strategy of achieving wealth and power through control of the land and peasantry. The second, motivated by domestic and international economic considerations, diversified its assets. With its wealth no longer tied to agriculture, its preferences in state economic policy and instruments of social control also changed (LeVine 1997; Wood 2000). The 1988 legislative victory of the *Alianza Repúblicana Nacionalista* (ARENA) and the election of ARENA's Alfredo Cristiani in 1989 marked the ascendancy of this second group (Pearce 1999). Under Cristiani, the Salvadoran government sought to rebuild and liberalize the economy while limiting the economic and military power of the Salvadoran military. A negotiated settlement of the conflict would serve both goals (Juhn 1998; Williams and Walter 1997).

Cristiani's ability to lead the Salvadoran government in negotiations with the FMLN was enhanced by changes in American foreign policy. Absent the logic of the Cold War and with intensified Congressional criticism of human rights violations by the Salvadoran Armed Forces (FAES) — especially following the 1989 murder of six Jesuit priests, their housekeeper, and her daughter — the US began to re-evaluate its Salvadoran policy. No longer willing to give Salvadoran authorities unquestioned support, the Bush administration increasingly linked foreign aid to respect of human rights and the rule of law. In August 1990 the US froze $19 million in military aid "making it clear that the decision could be reversed if the leadership of the FAES cooperated in the Jesuit case" (Byrne 1996, 181).

During this same period, the FMLN faced multiple challenges that increased the attractiveness of a negotiated settlement. Most significant were changes triggered by the financial collapse of the Soviet Union and end of the Cold War. Changes in Soviet foreign policy eliminated the Soviet Union as an actual or potential source of financial and military support as well as reduced Cuba's ability to provide aid to the FMLN. Political change in Nicaragua further reduced military and political support to the FMLN as well as eliminated safe havens for its fighters. Additionally, with no viable alternative to capitalism, the FMLN shifted its goals from socialist revolution to political reform and the creation of a social safety net within a capitalist economic system (Juhn 1998).

Fortunately for the Central American peace process, these events coincided with changes in how the international community understood its role in the resolution of civil conflict. Swept into what Linz and Stepan have referred to as the "democratically supportive *zeitgeist*" (1996, 74) of the era, many international actors came to advocate democratization as a strategy for the resolution of both international and civil conflict. They also proved willing to support democratic transitions with financial and technical assistance. United Nations peacebuilding developed as a tool through which the international community could actively support the negotiation and implementation of democratic transitions as part of a strategy to realize durable peace.

While these domestic and international factors enhanced the likelihood that a settlement could be negotiated, the success of the peace process in El Salvador was not guaranteed. UN peacebuilders played an important role in resolving El Salvador's civil war by helping to implement a peace treaty designed to enhance the quality and legitimacy of Salvadoran democracy. Finnemore and Sikkink's three-phase model of the social construction of norms parallels the negotiation and implementation phases of the Salvadoran peace process. By engaging in norm articulation and the social construction of norms supportive of liberal democracy, supporters of the Salvadoran peace process were able to overcome resistance during both the negotiation and implementation stages. In the Salvadoran case, strategic social construction proved to require two forms of assistance: coercive manipulation of resources that raised the cost of non-compliance and enabling assistance in the form of resources, technical assistance and monitoring that facilitated implementation of military, political, and economic provisions of the agreements. The fact that more than five years following the withdrawal of UN peacekeepers El Salvador has managed to avoid a relapse of large-scale political violence suggests that, under the right conditions and with appropriate support, international actors can facilitate the creation of a durable peace.

Articulating Democratic Norms of Political Legitimacy

The international community was relatively slow to involve itself in efforts to resolve El Salvador's civil war. The initial UN response to the outbreak of armed conflict was limited. Following the 1979 murder of Archbishop Romero, the General Assembly called for an investigation of human rights abuses and a halt to military aid (A/35/192). International efforts to actively aid conflict resolution did not begin until January 1983 when the presidents of Mexico, Venezuela, Colombia and Panama met to form the Contadora Group. Their goal was to resolve the many civil conflicts that threatened the peace and stability of the entire Central American region. In September 1983, the Contadora Group issued its 21-point "Document of Objectives," calling for democracy and national reconciliation, an end to support for armed groups engaged in cross-border attacks, reduction of foreign troops and advisors, and arms control (Purcell 1985; Omang 1983). They encouraged the leaders of El Salvador, Nicaragua, Guatemala, Costa Rica, and Honduras to adopt these principals as the basis of a regional peace process.

The Contadora initiative soon gained support in resolutions passed by the Security Council and the General Assembly. The General Assembly resolution specifically identified "the necessity of promoting the achievement of peace on a sound basis, which would make possible a genuine democratic process, respect for human rights, and economic and social development." (A/38/10) This relationship between peace, democracy, human rights, and development was also asserted in the Organization of American States' Managua Declaration of 1983. The Managua Declaration further recognized "the need to consolidate...democratic structures and systems which encourage freedom and social justice, safeguard human rights and favor progress." By the mid-1980s, the UN General Assembly, the UN Security Council, and the Organization of American States *all* advocated conflict resolution strategies rooted in democratization and respect for human rights, reinforcing the norms articulated in the Contadora process.

The efforts of the Contadora Group were enhanced when Argentina, Brazil, Peru, and Uruguay formed the Support Group in 1985. Members of both the Contadora Group and the Support Group encouraged the Central American presidents to accept the "Procedures for the establishment of a firm and lasting peace in Central America" (Esquipulas II). All five Central American presidents signed Esquipulas II on 7 August 1987. The document clearly identified the problem of regional security as having both international and domestic components. Internationally, signators pledged to terminate aid to irregular forces and to prevent the use of their nation's territory by those engaged in conflict in neighboring states. International verification and follow-up was to be coordinated by the Secretaries-General of the UN and OAS. This provision led to the creation of The United Nations Observer Group in Central America (ONUCA, 1989-1992), the first full-scale UN peace operation in the Western Hemisphere.[2] Its primary mandate was to patrol the borders of the five Central American states and monitor each government's compliance with the international components of Esquipulas II. As the Nicaraguan peace process evolved, ONUCA was also tasked to assist the verification and physical demobilization of armed groups in Nicaragua. In February 1990, Nicaragua became the first sovereign state in which the UN (with OAS and other international organizations) monitored elections.[3]

ONUCA had two important effects on the conflict in El Salvador. First, the Nicaraguan government's cooperation with the Central American peace process, including increased border monitoring, limited the FMLN's foreign material support. Without which, the costs of sustaining the conflict were significantly increased. Second, the potential for peace through negotiation and UN implementation assistance was clearly demonstrated to the Salvadoran parties (Bosch 1999). ONUCA and related operations in Nicaragua served as a model that allowed both sides in the Salvadoran conflict to better understand the UN's verification role and facilitated creation of a common vision of how the stalemate between the FMLN and the Salvadoran government might come to a mutually satisfactory end.

In addition to outlining principles and norms intended to improve relations between states in the region, Esquipulas II also served to articulate norms that would prove important to intra-state conflict resolution and the reform of domestic political relations. Signators agreed to work toward the creation of "an authentic democratic process, both pluralistic and participatory, which entails the promotion of social justice, [and] respect for human rights." Each president also pledged to participate in a process of national reconciliation through dialogue with opposition groups that laid down their weapons and accepted amnesty. Tentative talks between the Duarte administration and the FMLN began shortly after Esquipulas II was signed but the two sides made little progress in finding a political settlement. The FMLN, believing the government's offer to negotiate was the result of the ongoing military stalemate, refused to disarm prior to initiating formal negotiations. The FMLN also pressed its longstanding demand that it share power in a transitional government. Reiterating the longstanding argument that sharing power with an armed group that refused to participate in the political process would deny "the very essence of democracy" and make "a mockery of the mandate that the people have bestowed upon us," Duarte refused (Duarte 1990a, 179).

The pledges to further democratize Salvadoran society in Esquipulas II, however, were not entirely without effect. The 1984 electoral transition from the presidency of Alvaro Magaña to José Napoleón Duarte had already demonstrated that opposition parties could come to power through the electoral process. Formally exiled leftist politicians Rubén Zamora and Roberto Ungo returned to organize the centrist Democratic Convergence in November 1987. In anticipation of the 1988 National Assembly and 1989 presidential elections, centrist parties and ARENA increased electoral efforts indicating they had "come to accept a set of constitutional and electoral 'rules of the game'" (Baloyra 1998, 19).

It was in this atmosphere of repeated public pledges by the Duarte administration to create a more inclusive democracy that the FMLN presented its 12-point proposal in 1989. The FMLN pledged to disarm if it would be allowed to participate in upcoming national elections. It asked that the election date be postponed to 1990 so that it could have time to make security arrangements, and to organize and register supporters (Sciolino 1989; Torres-Rivas 1997, 223).[4] In an interview given at the time, FMLN Commander Joaquin Villalobos explained the FMLN's new position:

> By introducing the proposals, we are obviously playing with a totally new political design, one that constitutes a change from previous formulations for negotiations in which the FMLN has demanded its own positions of power. The FMLN now struggles for a more general demand more deeply felt by all forces: peace and democracy... (quoted in Lungo Uclés 1990, 163-164)

In this same interview, Villalobos also identified the need to "disassemble and purge" the army, security forces, and judicial system as part of the process of creating a functioning democracy in El Salvador. He called for greater tolerance of political debate and freedom of expression and an end to single-party rule. He argued that "there must be an internal political give-and-take combining the representative democracy of elections and parties with the permanent democracy of mass participation in the decisions of political, economical and social management" (quoted in Lungo Uclés 1990, 165). This sentiment was echoed by FMLN Leader Fermán Cienfugas who called for a system of "participatory" democracy and "ideological pluralism" (quoted in Lungo Uclés 1990, 165). Though the FMLN was not permitted to participate in the 1989 election (as it expected[5]), the proposal remained an important statement of its new bargaining position. In announcing its willingness to work within the electoral framework of the 1983 constitution, the FMLN gave up its long standing demand for formal power sharing and accepted the GOES demand that the FMLN disarm and compete for political power.

The 1989 presidential election allowed candidates to play the role of democratic norm entrepreneurs. ARENA's Alfredo Cristiani presented himself as *the* candidate able to attain peace in El Salvador through democratic reform of political and social structures. Cristiani proposed talks with rebel leaders and acknowledged the social roots of the conflict. He promised to increase spending on education and health care, to strengthen the justice system, to improve the government's land redistribution program, and to improve respect for human rights (Gruson 1989a; 1989b). On 7 August 1989, the five Central American presidents, including El Salvador's newly elected Cristiani, signed the Tela Declaration[6] in which they reaffirmed their commitment to the principles of Esquipulas II. The Tela Declaration specifically called upon the FMLN "to put an immediate and effective end to hostilities so that a dialogue may be carried out that will lead to rejection of armed struggle and the reintegration of the FMLN members into institutional and democratic life." In the Declaration's Annex, the Salvadoran government expressed "its unequivocal respect for its commitments to national reconciliation and to continuing strengthening the existing process of pluralistic, participatory and representative democratization by means of which social justice and full respect for all human rights and fundamental freedoms of Salvadorans is promoted."

The Security Council expressed support for Esquipulas II and encouraged the Secretary-General use his good offices to foster peace in Central America (S/RES/637). UN Secretary-General Javier Perez de Cuéllar was soon invited by both the FMLN and the Salvadoran government to send a representative to talks scheduled to take place in San José, Costa Rica from 16-17 October 1989. De Cuéllar appointed fellow Peruvian Alvaro de Soto as his personal representative. By this time the FMLN and the government of El Salvador both accepted the principles of civilian control of the military and the rule of law as important components of post-conflict Salvadoran society. Separately, they had both issued statements that equated political legitimacy with democratic governance understood as a representative government, elected under free and fair conditions, that ensured respect of human rights and the rule of law (Baloyra 1998, 28).

While the Salvadoran Government, the FMLN and external supporters of the peace process articulated a number of shared principles consistent with contemporary understandings of liberal democracy, the mechanisms for implementation and shape of final institutional structures remained contentious. Agreement on general principles was not enough to erase the legacy of distrust between the two sides, or their willingness to use the battlefield to affect outcomes at the negotiation table. The San José talks soon broke off with news that a prominent trade union leader was killed in an explosion in a union hall. The FMLN followed with the November 1989 offensive that for the first time brought the war directly to San Salvador. The violence that followed claimed hundreds of lives, but also re-affirmed for both sides the necessity of a negotiated settlement (Baloyra 1998).

The Central American Presidents responded to this new level of violence with "The Declaration of San Isidro de Coronado" of 12 December 1989. In it they expressed support for Cristiani as the leader of a government "established through democratic, pluralistic and participatory processes." They called upon the FMLN to renounce violence and end hostilities. Further, they requested the UN Secretary-General "do everything within his power to take the necessary steps to ensure resumption of the dialogue between the Government of El Salvador and the FMLN."[7] UN-mediated talks were renewed in February resulting in the Geneva Agreement of 4 April 1990.[8] The Geneva Agreement identified the goals of the Salvadoran peace process as not only an end to the armed conflict but also the reunification of Salvadoran society and the creation of a democratic political system that would respect and protect human rights. The Geneva Agreement was soon followed by the Caracas Agreement on 21 May 1990.[9] It established a two-phase agenda for future negotiations. Political issues including reform of the constitution, the armed forces, the judiciary, and the electoral system, as well as human rights, economic and social issues were to be settled prior to the formal end of hostilities. Resolution of the armed conflict itself was to take place in a second-phase of negotiations. These negotiations would include agreements on disarmament, demobilization and reintegration of forces as well as the reorganization of the FMLN as a legal political party.

The Road to Chapultepec

The first phase of norm construction continued as the FMLN, the Salvadoran government, and representatives of the UN Secretary-General began to work out the specific terms of settlement. Because the Geneva Agreement stipulated that negotiations would remain confidential except for public information provided by the UN Secretary-General or his representative, the process of further articulating democratic norms of political legitimacy took place at two levels. At the first level, representatives of the FMLN, representatives of the Salvadoran government, and de Soto and his staff from the UN Secretariat negotiated the terms of peace by applying and interpreting previously agreed principles of political legitimacy. This was not a negotiation over a division of spoils; it was a discus-

sion of which principles and norms should govern society and how they were to
be institutionalized. The discussion was about the nature of a *process* that would
produce, repeatedly over time, an *appropriate* and therefore legitimate outcome.

At the second level, the process of norm articulation was expanded to actors
not directly involved in the negotiations but nonetheless capable of significantly
supporting or hindering the peace process. External supporters of the peace
process, particularly the United States and the "Friends of the Secretary-
General" (Columbia, Mexico, Spain, and Venezuela) used pre-existing contacts
with the Salvadoran parties to support the social construction of peace (de Soto
1999). Internally, as those directly involved in the negotiations came to support
the peace process and specific treaty provisions, they faced the challenge of
convincing skeptical colleagues within their own parties as well as other members of Salvadoran civil society. After the Geneva Agreement was signed, the
Comisión Inter-Partidara (IP) was formed in an effort to provide a forum in
which all nine political parties represented in the Legislative Assembly could
meet and discuss the unfolding peace process.[10] Though not formally a party to
the negotiations, the IP "was critical to getting legislative support" without
which constitutional reforms necessary to implement the terms of the peace
could not have been approved (Juhn 1998, 58).

A parallel process was also created to gain military support for the peace
process. The government's military representative on the negotiating team was
Colonel Mauricio Vargas.

> [He] was responsible for keeping the armed forces informed of the progress of
> the negotiations, and for explaining proposed changes in a series of seminars
> for military officials that, supported by U.S. pressure, ensured that the changes
> were "less traumatic than they might have been."   (Byrne 1996, 189-190)

The military, the group that would be asked to give up the most in the peace
process, was the primary target of strategic social construction. As predicted in
Finnemore and Sikkink's model of norm construction, rhetorical appeal to
shared values was not enough to overcome resistance rooted in pre-existing
norms and interests. The need for a proactive policy of strategic norm construction was soon apparent as the relatively rapid progress of the Geneva and Caracas Agreements was followed by an impasse over the issue of military reform.

While off-the-record comments by US and Salvadoran government officials
identified military reform as "the FMLN's most potent and legitimate point"
(Byrne 1996, 182), the High Command insisted that the structure of the armed
forces was not subject to negotiation. The US facilitated strategic social construction in two important ways. First, the US utilized the 'Friends' mechanism
to preclude a military coup. In late May 1990, President Bush placed a call to
Venezuelan President Carlos Andrés Pérez asking him to convey the message
"that 'Cristiani cannot be removed neither by decree nor by coup'. Cristiani
would finish his term as president with the protection of the United States government." (Juhn 1998, 60) Second, the US used its position as El Salvador's

primary source of military aid to pressure the High Command to cooperate with the UN-led peace process. Congress voted to withhold half of the $85 million in military aid budgeted for fiscal 1991 while making clear the terms by which the funds would be released. These initiatives produced short-term strategic cooperation. By January, the High Command agreed (partially) to a UN-sponsored proposal for military reform. While it tentatively agreed to transfer police functions to the Ministry of Interior, to dismantle civil defense patrols, and to reduce the overall size of the armed forces, it rejected proposals to purge the officer corps and to merge FMLN and government forces. Once the Bush administration released the remaining funds in mid-January, the High Command reverted to its original position (Williams and Walter 1997).

Although the Caracas Agreement prioritized negotiations of the future status of the military, the continued resistance of the High Command required that other issues be addressed if the momentum of the peace process was to be sustained. In the absence of a military agreement, de Soto proposed an agreement on Human Rights. The subsequent San José Agreement on Human Rights was signed on 26 July 1990.[11] In it, both sides agreed to respect human rights as defined by Salvadoran law, international treaties to which El Salvador was a party, UN and OAS declarations, and other internationally recognized standards. The agreement also included provision for deployment of UN human rights monitors following the end of armed conflict. UN monitors were authorized to investigate reports of human rights violations and to make recommendations to improve protection of human rights and due process of law.

In some respects, an agreement on human rights was an easy target for early agreement. Building on the pledges of the Tela Declaration, the San José Agreement asked no more of the Salvadoran government than it reaffirm commitments to which it had already consented by virtue of its membership in the OAS and the UN and as a signator of international human rights treaties. The agreement also provided the Cristiani government with an opportunity to realize its own goals of reigning in the military and promoting the rule of law. The San José Agreement was also consistent with the FMLN's long-standing rhetorical claims, including those made following its 1989 12-point proposal. Both sides stood to benefit politically if they could convince voters that they should be credited with helping to reign in human rights abuses. Agreement was reached when publicly articulated normative values and interests overlapped. The extensive role of United Nations human rights monitors included in this agreement was also the result of this overlap of publicly stated normative values and interests. Both sides had already agreed to UN monitoring of *all* future agreements in the Geneva Agreement; human rights monitoring was a simple extension of this principal. Monitoring also served as a form of enabling aid; it protected both sides against potential cheating.

The Caracas Agreement set a target date of mid-September 1990 for the first phase of negotiations. September came and went with no further substantive agreements due primarily to the military's continued resistance to proposed reforms. Meanwhile, the Cristiani Administration made public statements to mark its continued support of the mediation process and the goals outlined in the Geneva Agreement. In the 17 December 1990 Declaration of Puntarenas,[12] the five Central American Presidents renewed their commitment to democracy and requested:

> the international community and the relevant specialized agencies to [sic] increase cooperation aimed at enhancing the functioning of the various branches of government and, in particular, improving the administrative and judiciary machinery guaranteeing the full observance of basic human rights.

The Central American Presidents also voiced support for the Secretary-General's efforts and expressed hope that a cease-fire agreement would soon be reached so that human rights monitors could be deployed.

The UN opened the Preparatory Office in San Salvador the following month. Its presence facilitated negotiations through logistical and other support and unofficially provided UN headquarters with information and analysis. Despite these efforts, negotiations stalled This became a source of concern for negotiators as they realized a peace strategy based on reform of the 1983 Salvadoran Constitution imposed its own deadline for agreement. The constitutional amendment process required approval of two consecutive Legislative Assemblies. Any constitutional reform resulting from the peace process would have to be approved by 30 April 1991. If that deadline was missed, the constitution could not be legally amended until 1994. The Mexico City Agreement met the 30 April deadline with just days to spare. The key provisions of this agreement include:

- Military Reform – Parties agreed to the principle of civilian control of the military. The National Civil Police (PNC) and the State Intelligence Agency would be created to eliminate the military's role in civil policing. Training of both the armed forces and civilian police would emphasize respect for human rights and democratic values.

- Judicial Reform – The post of National Counsel for the Defense of Human Rights was created. Election of Supreme Court Judges, the Attorney General and the National Counsel for the Defense of Human Rights would require support of two-thirds of the Legislative Assembly. The judiciary was guaranteed an annual allocation of at least six percent of the state budget. Reforms designed to improve professional standards and the independence of the judicial system were also included.

- Electoral Reform – The Supreme Electoral Tribunal would replace the Central Board of Elections. Electoral rolls were to be updated with the participation of all political parties.

- The Commission on the Truth – The parties agreed to create a three member panel (to be selected by the Secretary-General) to investigate "serious acts of violence that have occurred since 1980 and whose impact on society urgently requires that the public should know the truth."[13]

The outgoing Legislative Assembly approved nearly all amendments needed to implement the Mexico Agreement. Final enactment required the support of two-thirds of the new assembly.

Despite progress in many areas, negotiations to restructure the armed forces remained deadlocked (Williams and Walter 1997, 152). Once again, UN mediators sought progress on non-military matters to maintain momentum in the negotiation process. The Salvadoran government, the FMLN, and civil society groups expressed strong support for early deployment of monitors as called for in The San José Agreement on Human Rights. Both the FMLN and Salvadoran government agreed to protocols designed to ensure the safety of monitors despite the absence of a cease-fire agreement (LeVine 1997).

The United Nations Observer Mission in El Salvador (ONUSAL) was created by Security Council Resolution 693 on 20 May 1991, following the recommendation contained in "The Secretary-General's Report to the Security Council" of 21 December 1990 (S/22031). The report advised the Security Council that the Salvadoran government and the FMLN had requested human rights monitors be deployed "as soon as possible without waiting for other agreements to be concluded." It also anticipated future requests to monitor the March 1991 legislative and municipal elections, a cease-fire agreement, and implementation of other aspects of the peace process. Under its initial mandate, ONUSAL was to be deployed for a period of twelve months "to verify the compliance by the parties with the Agreement on Human Rights signed at San José on 26 July 1990." The Council reserved the right to approve "subsequent tasks or phases of the Observer Mission" (S/RES/693). Early deployment of UN monitors built confidence in the peace process as well as the role of the UN in it. Further, it helped build relationships that would facilitate the work of later ONUSAL divisions (LeVine 1997).

The Human Rights Division of ONUSAL initially deployed 26 July 1991 and became operational 1 October, at which time it began a process that the Director of the Human Rights Division, Diego Garcia-Sayan, labeled "active verification." Active verification consisted of a three-step procedure in which the Human Rights division received complaints, conducted investigations of reported abuses, and made recommendations to Salvadoran authorities. Activities were coordinated with the Salvadoran government, the FMLN, and human rights NGOs. Through the investigation of individual cases of human rights abuses, the Human Rights Division sought to reveal structural problems in the administration of justice and assertively pushed "for structural remedies to systematic human rights violations" (Johnstone 1995, 26). In the process of doing their work, human rights monitors facilitated the social construction of new norms. Negative reports could trigger denial of aid by donors. Monitors also provided enabling aid in the form of technical assistance and observation, which facilitated implementation of the San José Agreement and reduced overall insecurity.

Further support for the Salvadoran peace process came out of the new cooperative relationship between the US and USSR. On 1 August 1991, representatives of the two governments issued a joint statement expressing support for the Secretary-General's efforts to promote peace in El Salvador. The same day, in a letter addressed to the Secretary-General, the Soviet Minister of Foreign Affairs and the US Secretary of State noted:

> The United States and the Soviet Union are prepared to extend full cooperation to this intensified effort in the context of the Security Council and bilaterally. We offer to join together with you and the Friends of the Secretary-General to cooperate with a new negotiating round on an intensive basis so that we might offer our full support to help bring the parties to a resolution and help overcome any difficulties.   (S/22947)

This was a clear message that the two powers were prepared to engage in strategic social construction to advance the UN-mediated peace process.

The Secretary-General quickly invited President Cristiani and the FMLN Commanders to New York. The September 1991 talks resulted in agreement on a number of areas. The key provisions of the New York Agreement include:

- The National Commission for the Consolidation of Peace (COPAZ) – COPAZ was to be composed of two representatives from the government (one of which was to be a member of the armed forces), two representatives of the FMLN, and one from each of the six political parties represented in the Legislative Assembly. The Archbishop of San Salvador and ONUSAL could each designate one observer. COPAZ was to be "responsible for overseeing the implementation of all the political agreements reached by the parties" and "to issue conclusions and recommendations" (including draft legislation) with approval of a simple majority of voting members.

- The Ad Hoc Commission for Purification of the Armed Forces – The Ad Hoc Commission was to "purify" the armed forces, reduce its size, and redefine the role of the military in Salvadoran society. The Commission was to include members of the military who would have access only to deliberations. Further details relating to the Ad Hoc Commission were to be addressed in the compressed negotiations.

- The National Civil Police (PNC) – The PNC would replace the existing National Police force and take over domestic policing functions from the Salvadoran Armed Forces and State Intelligence Agency.

- Land Reform – Land reform would take place in the form of redistribution (primarily to former combatants) of lands to be acquired by government enforcement of constitutional limits on land ownership (245 hectares) and government purchase. Current land tenure in the conflict zones would be respected until a long-term settlement could be approved by COPAZ.

• Compressed Negotiations – Outstanding issues including reform of the armed forces, intelligence services, judiciary, and electoral system, as well as the cease-fire, disarmament and demobilization were to be negotiated simultaneously in the next round of talks.[14]

The New York Agreement was the product of hard bargaining between the parties. COPAZ was accepted by the Salvadoran government only if presented *"not as power sharing but as a matter of guarantees for the FMLN"* (Levine 1997, 240-241) and only after the FMLN agreed to dismantle its military structure and transform itself into a political party (Baranyi and North, 1996, 18). In exchange, the Salvadoran government agreed to create a new national police force and purge the military.

Cristiani was bitterly criticized for accepting the terms of the New York Agreement by conservative elements in Salvadoran society. A campaign of intimidation against ONUSAL personnel, the international press, local non-governmental organizations, and church groups supportive of the peace process began soon after the New York Agreements were signed (Baranyi and North 1996, 13). Despite this opposition, the peace process continued buoyed by even greater demonstrations of domestic and international support. The Security Council passed Resolution 714 in which it offered congratulations and encouraged further progress at the compressed negotiations. The FMLN declared a unilateral truce on 16 November. The government responded with a similar declaration in December. A formal cease-fire and separation of forces agreement soon followed.

The New York Act I was signed in the last seconds of de Cuellar's term as Secretary-General on 31 December 1991. In addition to cease-fire and separation of forces agreements, it included agreement on the creation of the National Civil Police. Perhaps the most remarkable aspect of the New York Act I was the provision that the newly appointed Secretary-General Boutros Boutros-Ghali propose "a formula for resolving outstanding issues," not resolved by 10 January. This procedure contributed to the New York Act II of 13 January 1992 which addressed all outstanding issues (Baranyi and North 1996).[15]

The final peace treaty, the Chapultepec Accords, was signed at a formal ceremony at Chapultepec Castle, Mexico City on 16 January 1992.[16] Combining all of the previous agreements between the FMLN and the Salvadoran government, the treaty was the product of a cumulative process of the articulation of norms appropriate to liberal democracy. Building on norms embodied in the Salvadoran Constitution of 1983 as well as public statements and commitments made by both the FMLN and the Government of El Salvador, the UN's lead negotiator Alvaro de Soto was able shepherd the parties through the negotiations. In the process, they created a shared vision of political legitimacy rooted in internationally accepted democratic standards. Despite representing the culmination of a three-year negotiation process, the Chapultepec Accords marked only the first steps down what would prove to be a long and difficult path. Efforts to implement the accords produced a number of crises that resulted in the return of political violence in other cases. With the support of the UN Secretariat, the Friends of the Secretary-General, the United States and other external supporters of the peace process, United Nations peacebuilders helped to implement the peace accords. By engaging in articulation and strategic social construction of norms supportive of liberal democracy, UN peacebuilders helped create a durable, self-sustaining peace in El Salvador.

Implementing the Chapultepec Accords

Negotiated settlements to end civil conflict often prove as difficult to implement as they are to negotiate. Many of the factors that make it difficult to reach a negotiated settlement remain present during the implementation phase of the peace process. Therefore, just as third-party mediation is often crucial to reaching a negotiated settlement, third-party support is also critical to the successful implementation or peace accords. Peacebuilders in El Salvador supported the implementation phase of the peace process by continuing to articulate norms consistent with the demilitarization of Salvadoran society and the establishment of a pluralist, liberal democracy. ONUSAL played a special role as authoritative interpreter of the accords and judge of each party's compliance with them. Peacebuilders further supported implementation of the peace accords through a process of strategic social construction. Coercive aid rewarded cooperation or punished non-compliance. Enabling aid, including monitoring, technical support and other forms of assistance, was made available to improve each side's capacity to fulfill its obligations as required by the peace accords. Foreign aid was particularly significant to the implementation of the Chapultepec Accords because it was the primary source of financing for many programs mandated by the peace process (Boyce 1995).

Initially, implementation of the Chapultepec Accords went smoothly. By the end of January, El Salvador's Legislative Assembly passed an amnesty law which allowed FMLN leaders to legally re-enter the country thus, clearing the way for the FMLN's reorganization as a political party. In anticipation of the formal cease-fire scheduled to begin 1 February 1992, the Security Council deployed 368 military observers. By late May, an additional 304 civilian police observers were in place throughout the country (Boutros-Ghali 1995b, 25). However, it was not long before UN peacebuilders faced their first major challenge. This and later crises during the implementation process were overcome by strategic social construction which facilitated the parties' willingness to allow ONUSAL to participate in the peace process "beyond the specific provisions in the accords" (Holiday and Stanley 1993, 421). This willingness to modify the implementation process according to the spirit if not the letter of the accords provided the flexibility needed to manage the implementation process in a way that contributed to the overall durability of the transition.

Violations of the peace accords often derive from one of four sources: outright defiance, insecurity, misinterpretation, and material or technical incapacity. The perceptions of violation by one side often trigger retaliatory non-compliance by the other. In the case of the Salvadoran peace process, the first major implementation crisis was triggered by a combination of these factors. As is often the case, the implementation of the military provisions of the accords was particularly sensitive in El Salvador. The transition process called for not only the demobilization and disarmament of the FMLN, but also the demilitarization of Salvadoran society as a whole. Combatants from both sides required to participate in a demobilization process so that they could be reintegrated into civilian society. The military, political, and economic provisions of the accords were sequentially integrated which meant that delays or changes to the demobilization process affected or could be affected by changes in other provisions of the accords including military reform, land reform, deployment of the national civil police, and political reform. Delayed or incomplete implementation of the military provisions of the accords threatened to unravel the entire peace process.

The first major challenge to the implementation of the Chapultepec Accords occurred when both sides missed the deadline for the first phase of cantonment set for 2 March 1992. While the majority of government troops were concentrated at approved sites, military personnel remained in several additional locations. The government argued both that the designated areas did not have sufficient capacity to accommodate all personnel required to participate in the first phase of cantonment and that the non-approved sites were of national importance and required protection. The government also accused the FMLN of not complying with its obligations under the first phase of the cantonment process and of filing incomplete weapons inventories. The FMLN denied its weapons inventories were inaccurate and argued that it was unable to complete the first phase of cantonment due to inadequate infrastructure in designated areas (Williams and Walter 1997). The FMLN was also expressed concern that the Salvadoran military had not fully complied with its obligations under the first phase of cantonment.

UN peacebuilders utilized a variety of strategies to gain acceptable levels of compliance from both sides. Diplomats invoked the terms of the accords and the normative framework of the peace process to urge both sides comply. Enabling aid was also employed. ONUSAL worked with the UN Development Programme, the World Food Programme, UNESCO, and other donors to improve living and sanitation conditions at the FMLN's designated cantonment sites. In an effort to improve communication between the parties and reduce insecurity and improve confidence in the peace process, UN military observers were attached to the cantonment areas. This allowed ONUSAL to engage in direct monitoring and reporting which increased the trust the parties put in the verification process and reassured "both sides of the sustainability of the cease-fire" (McCormick 1997, 285). In addition, mixed military working groups were established to enhance communication and facilitate problem solving. Chaired by an ONUSAL military observer and composed of representatives from both the Salvadoran and FMLN armed forces, the working groups met to overcome disagreements that arose over the implementation of the accords. When the Salvadorans could not reach agreement, the ONUSAL observer's proposal was usually accepted (sometimes despite a recorded formal objection by one of the sides[17]).

The crisis triggered by the failure to meet the deadline for the first phase of cantonment was soon followed by disagreement over the National Guard and Treasury Police. The Chapultepec Accords provided that, "The National Guard and the Treasury Police shall be abolished as public security forces and their members shall be incorporated into the army." (A/46/864-S/23501, Ch. 1, Sect. 6, Para. C) Initially, the Salvadoran government renamed the units and incorporated into the army structurally intact. The FMLN accused the government of failing to dissolve the two entities as required by the accords. It refused to fully demobilize its first group of combatants until the "illegal" bodies had been disbanded. In the government's defense, General Mauricio Vargas and other members of the High Command argued that the accords did not *require* the organizational dissolution of these bodies but only "the suppression of the security forces in their public security functions" (quoted in Williams and Walter 1997, 154). The government accused the FMLN of violating the accords with its refusal to fully demobilize its first group of combatants. At the request of both parties, UN Under-secretary for Peacekeeping Marrack Goulding mediated talks which resulted in agreement to repeal the law that created the two 'illegal' security forces. The implementation timetable was also adjusted (Williams and Walter 1997, 154). The willingness of both sides to allow UN personnel to serve as "authoritative interpreters" (Stanley and Holiday 1997, 26) of the accords facilitated the resolution of this situation and kept the entire peace process on track.

The degree to which Salvadoran society could be demilitarized, however, was limited by the capacity to implement other provisions of the peace accords. Demobilized soldiers needed to be reintegrated into civilian society. Reintegration could succeed only if former combatants were provided with an alternate source of income. Former combatants were designated as the primary beneficiaries of the land reform program; the success of demobilization would depend on the capacity of the land reform program to provide an alternative livelihood for decommissioned soldiers. Under the Chapultepec agreement, the Salvadoran government agreed to acquire land for the program through three sources: transfer of government owned land; enforcement of constitutional limits on private land ownership; and purchase of private land sold voluntarily at market prices. Former combatants and other program beneficiaries would be allowed to purchase land "at market prices." Purchases were funded through "fixed price and long-term financing at low, fixed interest rates not subject to interest capitalization" (A/46/864-S/23501, Ch. V, Sect. 2.E).[18]

To facilitate implementation of this and other provisions of the accords, The National Commission for the Consolidation of Peace (COPAZ) was created.

Among its other duties, COPAZ was specifically tasked with working out the details of implementing legislation for the land reform program. However, COPAZ's structure contributed to its inability to perform the functions envisioned for it in the Accords. Delegates representing the National Conciliation Party, the Authentic Christian Movement, and ARENA frequently sided with the government while Democratic Convergence, the Christian Democratic Party, and the National Democratic Union sided with the FMLN (Baranyi and North 1996, 18). With neither side able to gain a majority, COPAZ was frequently deadlocked. Without implementing legislation the land reform program stalled triggering delays in the demobilization of both government and FMLN forces and threatening the entire peace process.

Pressure not to miss the planting season led some to take matters into their own hands in February and March of 1992. In violation of the accords, peasant groups seized property and were subsequently evicted by government security forces. Goulding was again dispatched to El Salvador to find a solution to the crisis. Working from the principles laid out in the Chapultepec Accords, Goulding persuaded the parties to end land seizures and evictions. Additional consultative mechanisms were created while COPAZ remained formally tasked with reaching agreement on a long-term policy. In addition, the UN Secretary-General provided enabling assistance. Consulting experts from the International Monetary Fund (IMF), the World Bank, and the Food and Agricultural Organization (FAO), and drawing on the input of the FMLN and the Salvadoran government, Boutros-Ghali proposed his own solution. Program beneficiaries would repay loans over 30 years (with a 4-year grace period) at an annual interest rate of 6 percent (S/25812). This proposal was soon accepted along with a revised implementation timetable (Boutros-Ghali 1995b).

The implementation process did not stay on-track for long. With demobilization already behind schedule additional disputes arose over the Ad Hoc Commission. The Commission was to identify members of the Salvadoran armed forces responsible for some of the war's worst atrocities. It was composed of three Salvadoran civilians "of recognized independence of judgment and unimpeachable democratic credentials" and "two officers of the armed forces with impeccable professional records." The military members of the Commission were barred from any access to the investigative process itself but were allowed to participate in other aspects of the Commission's work. Installed on 16 May 1992 the commission was charged with the overwhelming task of reviewing over 2,000 files in just three months (Holiday and Stanley 1993, 425).

While the recommendations of the Ad Hoc Commission were intended to be confidential, a preliminary draft of the commission's report was leaked in early September. It identified 102 officers to be purged including the minister and vice-minister of defense and most generals and colonels (Holiday and Stanley 1993; Bosch 1999). The official report, submitted to Boutros-Ghali and Cristiani on 22 September, included this same recommendation. The accords gave the Salvadoran government only one month to complete implementation. From the time it was leaked, Cristiani faced fierce resistance from within the

Salvadoran establishment. High ranking officers publicly criticized the report as "a leftist plot to decapitate the military" (Holiday and Stanley 1993, 425). The right wing press labeled the report "illegal and characterized it as an attempt by foreigners to undermine Salvadoran sovereignty" (O'Shaughnessy and Dodson 1999, 106).[19] The Salvadoran government soon announced (contrary to the provisions of the peace accords) that the Commission's recommendations would be implemented only after the complete demobilization of the FMLN.

The FMLN was divided in its response. Given El Salvador's history of military involvement in politics, The People's Revolutionary Party and the National Resistance "were quite concerned about making President Cristiani's position *vis-à-vis* the military untenable and therefore displayed more flexibility than the other FMLN factions." (Johnstone 1997, 317) Joaquín Villalobos, for example, sought to bargain with Cristiani. He offered to accept "postponement of the full implementation of the Ad Hoc Commission recommendations until the end of Cristiani's term in office in June 1994" in exchange for "assurances of greater security and resources for FMLN leaders and supporters" (Baranyi and North 1996, 23). When this offer became public, it was denounced by competing factions within the FMLN as well as civil society organizations, and human rights groups. These groups expressed concern that incomplete compliance with the Ad Hoc Commission report would undermine efforts to reform the military and subordinate it to civilian control (Baranyi and North 1996, 24). In the end, the FMLN postponed demobilization of the last 40 percent of its forces pending government compliance with the Commission's recommendations (Williams and Walter 1997, 226n17).

Meanwhile, representatives of the UN Secretariat and ONUSAL continued to press for full implementation of the Ad Hoc Commission's recommendations. The Secretary-General and his representatives, the Friends of the Secretary-General (especially Colombia, Mexico, Spain, and Venezuela), and the United States repeated the message that anything less than full compliance was unacceptable. UN representatives refused "to compromise on [aspects] of the Accords that it viewed as essential to the legitimacy and sustainability of the peace process" (McCormick 1997, 294). The US, in particular, "facilitated progress by remaining uniformly committed to the position of the Secretary-General and providing reassurances to the Cristiani government" (McCormick 1997, 294). This message was emphasized on 15 November 1992 when (then) US General Colin Powell met with Cristiani and the High Command and encouraged they find a "workable solution" (McCormick 1997, 294). Goulding and de Soto continued to demand full compliance and worked with the Cristiani administration on an agreement in which most of the Commission's recommendations were incorporated in the year-end general orders.

In an effort to put the process back on schedule ONUSAL certified the FMLN's demobilization complete on 14 December 1992, despite its own misgivings and government protests (McCormick 1997; Stanley and Holiday 1997). This cleared the path for the recognition of the FMLN as a legal political party, paving the way for its participation in the March 1994 elections. A ceremony commemorating the end of the first phase of implementation was held in San Salvador the following day, dubbed National Reconciliation Day. President Cristiani used the occasion to announce that with the end of the armed conflict, "there is only one way open to settle political differences: political institutionality." He declared that all of Salvadoran society was united around the goal of "the democratization of our institutions" (1993). Citing progress in constitutional and military reform, the creation of a new electoral code, and the registration of the FMLN as a legal political party, Schafik Hándal, Secretary-General of the FMLN, concurred, "We have now ended the armed peace and are beginning the civic, political struggle, which marks even more significant progress [of seeking reconciliation] for the sake of stability, peace, and democracy" (Hándal 1993).

The governments of Colombia, Mexico, Spain, Venezuela, and the United States used this occasion to issue a joint statement declaring their intention to continue "efforts to gain the support of the international community for the important process of national reconciliation and reconstruction in El Salvador, within the framework of the attainment of democracy, peace, stability and the development of all Central America" (A/47/842-S/25007). Later that month, a US-Soviet joint-statement congratulated the parties for their progress and, "reiterate[d] their readiness to continue to assist in this effort and express[ed] hope that other interested States and international and regional organizations will offer their support" (A/47/853-S/25056). These statements supported construction of democratic norms of political legitimacy by explicitly linking these values to foreign aid. Aid conditionality in which the reports and statements of ONUSAL and the UN Secretary-General were used to determine compliance facilitated the implementation of the peace accords.

In early January 1993, Cristiani formally announced plans for the phased retirement of 87 of the officers identified in the Ad Hoc Commission report. The remaining fifteen officers, including Minister of Defense Ponce and Vice Minister of Defense Zepeda were to retire at the end of Cristiani's term in May 1994 (Williams and Walter 1997). Cristiani also invited the United Nations to observe the March 1994 elections. In a 7 January 1993 letter to the Security Council, Boutros-Ghali indicated his willingness to accept Cristiani's proposal as complying with the Ad Hoc Committees recommendations with the exception of the 15 senior officers who were to remain in place to the end of Cristiani's term. The Secretary-General and his representatives, the Friends of the Secretary-General, and the United States continued to press for full compliance. Public urging turned to coercive inducement in February 1993 when the Clinton administration froze $11 million in military aid. Aid would be released only when the Secretary-General accepted the government's compliance with *all* aspects of the Ad Hoc Commission's recommendations (McCormick 1997, 294).

Efforts to induce compliance with the Ad Hoc Commission's recommendations were augmented when the Truth Commission's report "From Madness to Hope: the 12-year war in El Salvador" was released in March 1993.[20] Under the accords, the Truth Commission was charged with investigating "serious acts of violence ... whose impact on society urgently requires that the public should know the truth." (A/46/553-S/23130) The Truth Commission differed from the Ad Hoc Commission in that its mandate was more expansive and its findings and recommendations would be public. Eighty-five percent of the cases it reviewed involved "state agents, paramilitary groups, or death squads allied with official forces" (Americas Watch 1993, 3). ARENA party founder, Major Roberto D'Aubuisson, was identified as ordering the 1979 assassination of Archbishop Oscar Romero. The report also cited "substantial proof" that Minister of Defense Ponce was behind the murder of six Jesuit priests at Central American University in 1989. Other senior military officers and judicial authorities were identified as authorizing or covering up human rights violations. The report further warned of the continued existence of death squads linked to state intelligence and security agencies (Baranyi and North 1996, 45). The FMLN was found responsible for five percent of the cases examined, including the murder of eleven mayors (Americas Watch 1993, 3).

The Truth Commission did not recommend prosecution of those identified in its report because in its opinion El Salvador's justice system did not meet "the minimum requirements of objectivity and impartiality" (S/25500). Instead, it recommended that some individuals be dismissed from public office and that others be disqualified from holding public office for a period of at least 10 years. It also called for the immediate resignation of the entire Supreme Court. The Truth Commission suggested additional remedies that might lead to the creation of "a democratic society in which the rule of law prevails and human rights are fully respected and guaranteed." (S/25500) To this end, it called for a number of reforms that would lead to the creation of a professional and independent judiciary. It also called for complete implementation of the peace accords, including full implementation of the Ad Hoc Commission Report, reform of the armed forces, investigation of illegal groups, full deployment of the National Civil Police and implementation of the recommendations of ONUSAL's Human Rights Division.

While the FMLN expressed some reservations, it "accepted the [Truth Commission's] recommendations in their entirety" (Wilkinson 1993b, A16). In contrast, high ranking members of the Salvadoran judiciary and military were very critical. In a national television appearance aired simultaneously on all of El Salvador's television stations, General Ponce denounced the Commission's report as "unjust, incomplete, illegal, unethical, partial and insolent" (quoted in Montgomery 1995b, 243). Members of the Supreme Court "cited it as proof of the Truth Commission's overreaching and inappropriate attempt to violate the constitutional order and Salvadoran Sovereignty" (Bertram 1995, 393).[21] Supreme Court President Mauricio Gutiérrez Castro rejected the legal competence of the Truth Commission and "repeatedly expressed his opinion that the peace accords [did] not apply to the judiciary, since they were signed only by the executive branch of government and the FMLN" (Holiday and Stanley 1993, 424). He further declared, "The only one who can fire me is God." (Montgomery 1995b, 243; Bertram 1995, 393) Media reports at the time echoed the concerns of many that the accords would not be fully implemented. As one report noted, "While no one is predicting a coup, politicians, former guerilla leaders, and others expressed fears that the military's resistance would deal a dangerous setback to the peace process – and thus erode the president's authority" (Wilkinson 1993a).

In the face of severe criticism from members of his own party, the military and the judiciary, Cristiani argued that the method by which the Truth Commission conducted its investigation and its recommendations was inappropriate and possibly illegal under Salvadoran law. Writing to the Secretary-General on 30 March 1993, Cristiani noted the mandate for the Truth Commission specified, "The Commission shall not function in the manner of a judicial body." In his view the Commission did not have the authority "to judge, impose sanctions, classify criminal acts, or evaluate evidence." [22] Cristiani was most critical of the Commission's recommendation deemed contrary to Salvadoran law. He argued that the Salvadoran Constitution did not grant the executive branch authority to remove judges from the Supreme Court and that therefore, he could not comply. The Salvadoran Constitution required that legal reform be enacted by the National Assembly. Cristiani, however, did not reject of the Truth Commission's recommendations in their entirety. His letter concluded:

> [W]e will, within the sphere of our competence, comply strictly with the recommendations of the Commission on the Truth in so far as they are in accordance with the Constitution of the Republic, are in harmony with the Agreements resulting from the direct negotiations, contribute to the reconciliation of Salvadorian society and do not involve the exercise of any jurisdiction which infringes on our system and established institutional order.
>
> (reprinted in United Nations 1995a, 415)

Throughout this period, tensions remained high. While Salvadoran authorities resisted implementation of the Ad Hoc and Truth Commission recommendations and problems continued to plague the land program, the FMLN became less and less cooperative with the demobilization process. This in turn, was used by members of the military and other conservative elements in Salvadoran society to justify their own reluctance to implement some of the provisions of the accords. Each delay raised concerns that one of the sides would defect entirely. Amidst this atmosphere of uncertainty and distrust, an arms cache exploded in a Managua garage in May 1993. An ONUSAL investigation revealed 114 weapons depots "large enough to sustain operations for several years" in Nicaragua, El Salvador, and Honduras (Berdal 1993, 19).[23] The President of the Security Council labeled the discovery "the most serious violation to date of the commitments assumed under the peace accords" (S/25929). While most commentators were not surprised that the FMLN kept some weapons "as a kind of guarantee," (Stanley and Holiday 1997, 31) some were surprised that the caches included weapons as sophisticated as surface to air missiles (McCormick 1997, 287-287).[24]

The FPL (one of the FMLN's constituent groups) claimed responsibility for the arms caches. In a letter to the Secretary-General, the FPL's Sánchez Cerén explained that the FPL had not inventoried or destroyed all of its arms as required by the peace accords due to "its profound mistrust of the [Salvadoran] Armed Forces." (S/26005, para. 4)[25] This mistrust was amplified by delays in the peace process and the perception that the military was not committed to full implementation of its obligations under the accords. Sánchez Cerén's letter to the Secretary-General also featured a remarkable admission; "as [the] FMLN developed as a political party and its chances of expansion were increasing, the maintenance of those arms had become an onerous and unnecessary burden, incompatible with its new status." (S/26005, para. 4)[26]

Constructivists argue that identity is affected by environmental factors and that in turn identity shapes interest and subsequently political action. The process of norm construction described by Finnemore and Sikkink suggests that as norm entrepreneurs engage in norm articulation and strategic social construction, identities and interests will be adapted to fit the new socio-political environment. The FPL's statement seems to indicate that the process of norm construction was well on its way in June 1993. As the FMLN came to identify itself first and foremost as a democratic political party, the tools appropriate to its old identity as a guerilla movement became a liability. This new identity became possible only when gradual implementation of the peace accords, including the increased sense of security created by UN monitoring of cantonment, demobilization and other provisions of the accords, changed the relevant political calculus. The conditions of the new socio-political environment made the role of political party an increasingly appealing alternative. The FPL and the FMLN cooperated with ONUSAL's investigation and agreed to destroy the arms caches under ONUSAL supervision. The Salvadoran Government met its outstanding obligations to comply with the Ad Hoc Commission Report in July 1993 (S/26052). The cease-fire held and the FMLN retained its status as a legal political party.

With the crisis resolved, observers remained cautiously optimistic that the peace process would lead to a durable, self-sustaining peace. With the disarmament process complete, focus shifted to preparations for elections. Dubbed "The Elections of the Century" the elections scheduled for March 1994 would be the first to take place since the end of hostilities and the first in which the FMLN would participate. In addition, due to an unusual coincidence in the Salvadoran electoral cycle, the presidential, legislative and municipal elections all fell on the same date creating the potential for sweeping political changes at all levels of Salvadoran political life within the existing constitutional framework.

Despite the many changes brought about as part of the peace process, there was a great deal of concern that the conditions for free and fair election did not yet exist in El Salvador. The original implementation timetable assumed that the 1994 elections would take place in a country policed by the newly created National Civil Police (PNC). As elections approached, however, the PNC was not yet fully deployed and the old National Police remained in control of some areas. Initially, the PNC and ONUSAL had a cooperative relationship. The PNC had been the victim of slow implementation and inadequate resources. ONUSAL's civilian police division worked with the PNC providing training and logistical support (Spence, Vickers, and Dye 1995).

This cooperative relationship was reversed in mid-1993 with the appointment of new PNC head, Oscar Peña Duran. As one of those named in the Truth Commission Report, Peña Duran should not have been allowed to join the PNC and remained in office despite the protests of ONUSAL, the US, and many domestic actors. He began his tenure by refusing further technical and logistical support from ONUSAL (McCormick 1997). The PNC proved unable or unwilling to investigate and prosecute prominent suspects and suffered from eroding discipline and continued infiltration by those who opposed its doctrine and mission (McCormick 1997, 304). Human rights abuses and criminal acts including "a return to the use of torture, the excessive use of force, arbitrary detentions, and executions" increased following his appointment (Williams and Walter 1997, 175). Perhaps most serious to the future of the peace process was a string of political murders. Francisco Velis, member of the FMLN National Council and candidate in the forthcoming elections, and Elano Castro, member of the FMLN National Council, were killed in late 1993 along with several FMLN supporters. Supporters of conservative parties were also victims of political violence during this period; one member of ARENA and two former municipal officials were killed. Perhaps most concerning of all was the report by UN human rights monitors that these and other human rights violations "continue to be left without investigation" (Diamond 1996, 73)

Criticism from ONUSAL's Human Rights Division and the UN Secretary-General led to the joint request by Cristiani and the FMLN that foreign experts work in cooperation with local officials to support the investigation of these murders (Hampson 1996b, 92; Williams and Walter 1997). The Joint Group for the Investigation of Politically Motivated Illegal Armed Groups issued its report on 28 July 1994 (S/1994/989). It concluded that,

> despite the great strides in the process of pacification and the efforts made by Salvadorian society to consolidate a climate of national reconciliation, there still exist data that support the well founded suspicion that recourse to violence in order to solve political differences has not yet been definitively eradicated.
>
> (S/1994/989, Annex para. 14)

Most of the violence was characterized as "private political violence" (i.e., acts of violence that are politically motivated but neither criminal structures nor agents of the State play a role in their commission). Retribution was identified as the primary motive (S/1994/989, para.13).

The Report by ONUSAL's Human Rights Division covering the period from 1 August to 31 October 1993[27] included its own analysis of suspected political assassinations and death squad activity. It found "widespread [...] deterioration of the human rights situation" and increased activity of illegal armed groups (death squads) coinciding with the start of the formal electoral period and the final phase of the implementation of the peace accords. The Report, however, found significant differences between this violence and that which El Salvador had experienced throughout the 1980s. At that time, death squad activities were

> directed against broad social sectors and political groupings... when one group defended the established system and the other fought to change it. That situation was expressly resolved by the peace agreements, through the constitutional, political and institutional reforms that the parties formerly in conflict agreed to by consensus, with the support of all other political forces.
> (A/49/59-S/1994/47, para.15)

In contrast, the new wave of violence

> is directed against the democratic political system which has been worked out by the Government and the FMLN, with the support of all political forces, with the aim of building up through consensus the rule of law and a stable and functioning democracy.   (A/49/59-S/1994/47, para.16)

The report positively highlighted the government's actions not only to publicly condemn acts of political violence but also to take "a number of decisions that demonstrate the political will of the President of the Republic to investigate each case and mete out appropriate punishment to those found responsible for violations." It cited as examples creation of The Joint Group for the Investigation of Politically Motivated Illegal Armed Groups and cooperation by government officials in its investigation. The report concluded that political violence was rejected "by the Government and all political parties, the Catholic Church, nongovernmental organisations, labour organizations and trade unions" (A/49/59-S/1994/47, para.17).

Escalating violence led to increased pressure for complete implementation of the Truth Commission's recommendations. Peacebuilders responded with norm articulation as well as enabling and coercive uses of aid to support implementation of the Truth Commission's recommendations. United Nations legal experts conducted a detailed analysis of the Truth Commission report with respect to both the commission's mandate and the Salvadoran Constitution. It concluded that the recommendations conformed to both and that most could be legally implemented prior to the March elections. The Secretary-General and his representatives then appealed to potential donors to condition aid on the Salvadoran government's compliance with the Truth Commission's recommendations. "Donors ... made clear that future economic assistance [was] linked to compliance with Truth Commission recommendations." (Baranyi and North 1996, 46) The US Secretary of State "appointed a panel to examine the implications of the U.N.-sponsored El Salvador Truth Commission report for the conduct of U.S. foreign policy and the operations of the Department of State" (Baranyi and North 1996, 46).

Despite incomplete implementation of the accords and concerns that the conditions for free and fair elections were not present in El Salvador, the official campaign period began on 20 November. ONUSAL observers attended political rallies and met with Salvadoran election officials and political party representatives to verify compliance with the electoral code. On 5 November 1993, the Secretary-General's Special Representative, Augusto Ramirez-Ocampo, obtained signatures by six of the seven presidential candidates to the "Commitment of the presidential candidates to peace and stability in El Salvador," which included a pledge to maintain the "constructive evolution of the peace process and to implement all the commitments contained in the Peace Accords and rejected any politically motivated violence or intimidation" (S/26790, para. 92). The one candidate who did not sign declined because in his opinion the statement did not go far enough (S/26790, para. 92). While progress in the peace process was acknowledged by the Security Council later than month, it also took the opportunity to continue the process of norm construction by urging "all States, as well as the international institutions engaged in the field of development and finance, to contribute promptly and generously to support of the implementation of all aspects of the peace accords" (S/RES/888, para. 12).

With preparations for elections in full swing, representatives of ONUSAL's electoral division visited every town in El Salvador to observe voter registration. When the electoral rolls were closed on 19 January 1994 an estimated 85 percent of the voting-age population had registered. The voter registration process was facilitated by expanding a previously existing UNHCR program to provide documentation (birth certificates, personal identity documents, and identity cards) to Salvadorans. Despite these efforts, more than 74,000 voter registration applicants (2.8 percent of the entire pool of voters, but 10.4 percent of potential voters in former zones of conflict) were not included on the electoral roll due to lack of appropriate documentation. Still, ONUSAL's support of the voter registration process is credited with helping to "avoid a serious threat to the legitimacy of the 1994 elections," thereby keeping the peace process on track (Stanley and Holiday 1997, 25).

Preparations for the Elections of the Century continued smoothly. On 10 March 1994, all of the presidential candidates met at ONUSAL headquarters to sign "a declaration in which they declared their rejection of violence and their commitment to respect the result of the elections and to comply with the Peace Accords" (S/1994/304). Representatives of political parties at all levels signed codes of conduct and periodically met with ONUSAL to voice complaints and overcome disagreements between the parties during the campaign (S/1994/304). By the March 1994 elections, "all key political actors accepted the legitimacy of the elections and the constitutionality of the regime" they would produce (O'Shaughnessy and Dodson 1999, 99).

Elections took place as scheduled on 20 March 1994 under the watchful eyes of 900 ONUSAL observers, 3,000 international observers, and monitors from El Salvador's political parties. The first elections since the end of hostilities took place with no serious incidents of violence or political intimidation. In addition to monitoring, ONUSAL took active measures to promote the actual and perceived fairness of the process. When Salvadoran election officials threatened to relocate four polling stations due to "security concerns" ONUSAL observers insisted Salvadoran election officials comply with existing electoral law and offered security and logistical support to prevent their closure. Relocation of these stations would have disproportionately affected FLMN supporters. ONUSAL and party representatives observed the official vote count while ONUSAL publicly announced its 'quick count' tallies in an effort to reassure the parties of the official count's accuracy.

Despite these efforts, the elections were far from perfect. Some voting stations opened late, the process was slow, and public transportation to polling sites was limited. More seriously, at least 25,000 voters (nearly 2 percent of the electorate) were denied their vote either because their name did not appear on the electoral rolls (despite having been issued an electoral identity card) or because someone had already voted in their name. In total, 55 percent of potential voters participated in the elections. This number was more than in previous elections but lower than had been expected. ONUSAL estimated that irregularities in the voting process did not affect the outcome of the presidential race but could have influenced some results in elections for the Assembly and the municipal councils. ARENA's Calderón Sol won 49.03 percent of the total vote. Rubén Zamora, the coalition candidate endorsed by the *Convergencia Democratica*, the FMLN, and the *Movimiento Nacional Revolucionario* received 24.9 percent of the vote. The remaining votes were split between five additional candidates. In the Legislative Assembly, ARENA won 39 seats, the FMLN 21, the PDC 18, the PCN 4, the CD 1, and the PMU 1. At the municipal level, ARENA won control of 206 municipalities, the PDC 29, the FMLN 16, the PCN 10 and MAC 1. The FMLN contested results in 37 districts but Salvadoran election officials left results unchanged despite formal complaints from ONUSAL. With no presidential candidate receiving a numerical majority, a run-off election was scheduled for 24 April. Calderón Sol won the second presidential ballot, defeating Rubén Zamora 68.35 percent to 31.65 percent.

El Salvador After the 1994 Elections

Armando Calderón Sol was inaugurated as El Salvador's first post-civil war president on 1 June 1994. The FMLN emerged as the second largest political force in El Salvador. Calderon Sol set the tone for post-civil war politics in his inaugural address:

We are building a new El Salvador, which is modern, democratic and participa-
tive. This demands legality, security, honesty, respect for each other, solidarity
and opening. The framework for our administration will be the constitution and
the laws, which we, the government and the governed, must all respect. Our objective is the full state of law that will guarantee the equality of all Salvadorans
before the law, making sure that this will be the golden rule of national coexis-
tence, without improper privileges or unjust exclusions. (Calderon Sol 1994)[28]

Once in office, Calderon Sol worked with the FMLN and ONUSAL to complete
implementation of the peace accords through regularly scheduled tripartite meetings and joint working groups (S/1994/1000). The key outstanding provisions of
the accords were reform of the judicial system, administration of public security,
and land reform. The newly elected Legislative Assembly completed the process
of reform, passing most of the constitutional amendments approved by the previous Assembly. With these amendments in place, the Assembly elected a new
Supreme Court and Supreme Court President (Johnstone 1997, 333). The Assembly also passed legislation designed to de-politicize and professionalize the
judiciary and assured it six percent of the state budget (O'Shaughnessy and
Dodson 1999).

Judicial reform, however, only partly remedied the culture of impunity that
had existed throughout the conflict. With the Ad Hoc Commission's recommendations fully implemented, the new leadership of the armed forces voiced support for full compliance with the peace accords (A/1994/1212, para. 25). At the
time of Calderon Sol's election, the PNC was not yet fully deployed. Peña
Duran remained head of the fledgling agency despite the protests of ONUSAL,
the US, and many domestic actors. With his tenure in office came a rise in human rights violations. The PNC proved unable or unwilling to investigate and
prosecute prominent suspects and suffered from eroding discipline and continued infiltration by those who opposed its doctrine and mission (McCormick
1997, 304). Though the overall level of political violence dropped dramatically
after the 1994 elections, assassinations continued with no perpetrators arrested
(Spence, Vickers, and Dye 1995). Peña Duran resigned in May 1994. Once in
office, Calderon Sol filled this and other vital posts with "[i]ndividuals committed to increasing the efficiency of the National Civil Police" (A/49/281-
S/1994/886, para. 128). With material and technical assistance from ONUSAL,
Spain, and the US, PNC units were deployed nationwide by October 1994
(Spence, Vickers, and Dye 1995).[29] This allowed the government to fully demobilize the National Police by year end (McCormick 1997). In addition, the
Calderon Sol administration publicly acknowledged the existence of organized
crime supported by high-ranking military and police officers (S/1994/1000). In
what one commentator described as "a sign of changing times in El Salvador"
(Dalton 1994), three military officers were arrested and charged with theft and
homicide for their role in a high profile bank robbery. Military officers were no
longer "untouchable" (Dalton 1994).

While progress was made in implementing the legal and security reforms called for in the accords, implementation of other provisions faced "flagging commitments by both sides" (Hampson 1996a, 169). The land-transfer program was one of the most delayed and least completely implemented provisions of the accords due in part to the program's expense, lack of political will, and technical problems associated with El Salvador's outdated legal and bureaucratic procedures (S/1994/1000). The use of market mechanism triggered significant rises in the cost of land forcing the Salvadoran Government and the FMLN to agree to reduce the number of beneficiaries. Concerns were also raised that those who did participate would be unable to meet their mortgage obligations without access to credit and significant technical assistance. The international community provided enabling aid to keep this aspect of the peace process on track. The United Nations and NGOs provided technical aid. The United States Agency for International Development provided $1 million to fund land purchases for demobilized FMLN forces and $31 million for FAES forces (S/1994/1000).[30]

Efforts to fully implement the Chapultepec Accords continued into the fall of 1994. Representatives of the GOES and FMLN signed a joint declaration on 4 October 1994[31] in which they pledged: 1) to ensure full compliance with all outstanding agreements no later than 30 April 1995; 2) to establish joint mechanisms with ONUSAL "to determine the specific measures necessary for the rapid fulfillment" of compliance with the Peace Accords; and 3) to work together to secure international aid to support peace related programs. As time passed, UN reports increasingly identified "lack of organization and expertise – a common phenomenon in developing countries – and, in some instances, lack of financing" (A/1994/1212, para. 25) as the primary cause of delay in the implementation of outstanding commitments. The long-term viability of many peace-related programs came to depend on the work of UN development agencies as well as NGOs and bilateral donors who provided technical and financial assistance (del Castillo 1997). ONUSAL continued to oversee implementation of the accords until the operation's mandate formally ended on 30 April 1995.

Despite significant progress, not all provisions of the Chapultepec Accords had been implemented and international observers remained concerned that El Salvador might relapse into renewed violence. The United Nations Observer Mission in El Salvador (MINUSAL) was created to carry on where ONUSAL left off. Consisting of 18 specialists in areas where full compliance was still pending: civilian policing, human rights, the land reform program, and reintegration of former combatants. Its efforts, like those of ONUSAL in the period following the election of Calderon Sol, were geared toward lobbying for further reform and development of Salvadoran institutions (Montgomery 1995a; Spence, Vickers, and Dye 1995). The six-person United Nations Office of Verification (ONUV) assumed verification tasks on 30 April 1996.

As the provisions of the Chapultepec Accords were implemented, the statements and actions of El Salvador's political leaders began to indicate that the web of norms supportive of liberal democracy – pluralism, free speech, political dialogue, negotiation and compromise, representation of all sectors of society, and non-use of political violence – were taking hold. Over time, behavior patterns that supported and helped replicate El Salvador's new norms of political legitimacy emerged beyond what could be accounted for by either enabling or coercive aid alone. Democratic norms of political legitimacy became increasingly self-sustaining. This relationship between the actor's perceived positive experience with the new norms and consensual acts to operate under the normative structures they created is emphasized in the Secretary-General's Report:

> Progress in the transition to democracy and the consolidation of a State governed by law called for in the El Salvador peace agreements can be seen in the clearly visible change in the country's political and social climate. A gradual expansion of opportunities seems to be convincing people that dialogue and consultation are legitimate democratic vehicles for social relations and the settlement of disputes and to be discrediting the use of violence at all levels. The result is an atmosphere of diminished tension and renewed calm within which the rights and freedoms of the individual can be exercised.
>
> (A/49/585-S/1994/1220, para.105)

Additional evidence that democratic norms of political legitimacy had taken hold can be found in El Salvador's 1997 elections. Legislative and mayoral elections were held as scheduled in March 1997. The FMLN won the mayoral race in San Salvador and 55 other cities. In the Legislative Assembly, the FMLN won 27 seats, just one less than ARENA (Miller 1999). Power sharing emerged with the smaller parties taking five of the eleven seats on the assembly's board of directors and six of the fourteen committee chairmanships (Darling 1997, A4). ARENA's Francisco Flores won the 1999 presidential elections in the first ballot. The election campaign was "largely devoid of personal and ideological attacks, the two parties have strikingly similar platforms, both pledging to fight crime and poverty and shore up weak political institutions" (Kovaleski 1999). That the civil war is now a firmly part of El Salvador's past is confirmed by interviews conducted in the ex-conflict zones. While "political fragmentation among community groups in the ex-conflict zones still runs deep, there was a general desire to reconcile political differences in favour of addressing immediate socioeconomic needs" (McIlwaine 1998, 665).

Constructing Peace in El Salvador

Despite delayed and incomplete implementation of the Chapultepec Accords, El Salvador has experienced durable, self-sustaining peace since ONUSAL's withdrawal in 1995. United Nations peacebuilders and other third-party supporters of El Salvador's peace process facilitated this transformation by helping to construct political norms that supported pluralist, liberal democracy and delegitimized political violence. While the end of the Cold War improved the chances that negotiations would take place, it did not guarantee that a negotiated settlement would be reached or that it would be successfully implemented. By adopting a strategy consistent with Finnemore and Sikkink's model of norm construction, ONUSAL and other third-party supporters helped to establish a self-sustaining peace in El Salvador.

Finnemore and Sikkink (1998)[32] argue that new normative systems can be created when norm entrepreneurs engage in a process of social construction. In the first phase of this process, norm entrepreneurs articulate new norms by defining them and advocating their adoption. In the second phase, norm entrepreneurs combine norm articulation with strategic social construction. In the short-term, strategic social construction reinforces new norms through aid conditionality such that cooperation is rewarded and non-compliance is punished. Over time, this reshapes the socio-political environment and with it the political calculus that governs decisionmaking. In the final phase, the new normative system becomes self-perpetuating as compliance becomes habitual. Once this occurs, the new norms can be described as self-sustaining and are expected to continue to influence behavior despite the withdrawal of coercive aid.

As Finnemore and Sikkink's model predicts, the construction of new political norms in El Salvador began with norm articulation. The Contadora Group was created in 1983 with the express purpose of advocating a regional peace strategy on the basis of democracy, human rights and national reconciliation. This approach was later endorsed by the Organization of American States as well as the UN General Assembly and Security Council. The creation of the Support Group in 1985 further reinforced these norms. Esquipulas II contributed to the peace process in both El Salvador and Nicaragua by defining the challenges to peace in the region and advocating a strategy of democracy, human rights and reconciliation to overcome them. The Nicaraguan peace process provided an important example which reassured the both sides that this formula combined with international assistance and monitoring could lead to a mutually acceptable transformation.

The formula for peace offered by the Contadora Group and the Support Group was relatively easy for the Salvadoran government to accept in part because it already identified itself as a democratic regime. In 1987 the Duarte administration signed Esquipulas II signaling its willingness to create a more inclusive democracy in El Salvador. The FMLN responded with its 12-point proposal in which it gave up its long-standing demand for power sharing and indicated its willingness to disarm prior to elections. This was followed by the 1989 Tela Declaration which reaffirmed the principles of Esquipulas II and specifically called on the FMLN reject armed conflict so that its members could be reintegrated into El Salvador's "institutional and democratic life." By the time Alvaro de Soto was named the UN Secretary-General's Special Representative, the Salvadoran parties had already signaled their willingness to accept the normative structure advocated by the Contadora Group and the Support Group as the basis of the Salvadoran peace process; peace would be the product of a negotiated settlement that would create a more inclusive democracy rooted in the rule of law and respect for human rights. Though it was significant that both sides accepted a loosely defined normative framework for the peace process, much work remained to transform relatively vague normative principles into a negotiated peace settlement.

Third-party mediation and support during the negotiation and implementation phases of the peace process was necessary to overcome the history of distrust and violence between the FMLN and the Salvadoran government. Third-party support was also particularly important in preventing the Salvadoran military and other armed conservative elements from playing the role of spoiler. Progress in UN mediated talks was "piecemeal." Each agreement represented only "what could and could not be agreed upon at a given time" (LeVine 1997, 228). The order of agreements, and later the order of implementation, reflected a hierarchy of shared values and interests. At the top were those issues in which one side made public commitments in advance of formal discussion. Second were agreements that could be justified as logical extensions of Salvadoran law, or pre-existing international commitments such as the early and rapid agreement to the San José Agreement on Human Rights. This agreement was accepted early in the process and was one of the first aspects of the accords to be implemented due, in part, to the fact that international and Salvadoran law combined to "legitimize and reinforce the parties' obligations of those aspects of the settlement" (Wilkins 1997, 256). When changes to Salvadoran law and institutions were accepted at the negotiation table, these changes were implemented through the amendment procedure of El Salvador's 1983 constitution. This procedure allowed significant change in El Salvador's institutions, particularly the judiciary and police force, in a way that conservative critics of the peace process could accept as legitimate.

More serious challenges to the peace process came from the military and other armed groups. State and non-state actors worked to support the peace process by overcoming challenges within the Contadora framework. They articulated a consistent vision of post-conflict society, the strategy by which it would be realized, and most importantly proved willing to engage in strategic social construction to realize this goal. The United States, historically the Salvadoran government largest sponsor, played a particularly important role in using this aid to leverage cooperation from El Salvador's military and civilian leaders. When negotiations bogged down over the issue of military reform in 1990 and again during the 1992 crisis over implementation of the Ad Hoc and Truth Commissions' recommendations, the United States withheld aid as part of a strategic social construction.

Enabling aid in the form of monitoring, technical assistance and financial aid which facilitated implementation of critical aspects of the accords and encouraged confidence in the peace process as a whole was also very important to the process of strategic social construction. For example, demobilization of FMLN forces depended upon aid provided by the United Nations Development Programme, the World Food Programme, the United Nations Economic and Social Council among others. Financial contributions from the United States and Spain provided training for the Civil National Police (S/23999). In his 23 November 1993 report to the Security Council, Boutros-Ghali acknowledged the role of aid conditionality played in the implementation process. He noted that donors engaged in coercive aid conditionality in which compliance with the peace accords was a necessary condition for the extension of aid. He also encouraged compliance as part of a strategy to acquire further enabling aid:

> Full compliance with the Peace Accords will strengthen my efforts to obtain external financial assistance in support of peace-related programmes. The parties must show a continued commitment to the rapid implementation of these programmes in order to sustain the interest and support of the international community. A third factor that could stimulate external support would be a clear demonstration of the Government's political will by giving these programmes the high priority they deserve and require in its budget.
>
> (S/26790, para. 91)

Though international financial assistance was the primary source of funding for many provisions of the peace accords, some analysts expressed concern that peace was undermined by international financial institutions that encouraged cuts in public spending and other economic reforms which adversely affected the implementation process. At times, contradictory demands from different sectors of the international community seemed to give the Salvadoran government mixed message and effectively restricted access to some resources that might otherwise have been available for fuller implementation of the peace accords.[33]

Despite some inconsistencies, donor acceptance of the principle of aid conditionality and willingness to allow the UN to serve as final arbitrar of compliance furthered the process of strategic social construction by providing a consistent interpretation of the accords as well as a predictable structure that rewarded compliance and punished noncompliance. By creating a "credible link between funding and the conditions embodied in formal commitments and informal policy dialogues" (Boyce 1995, 2113) peacebuilders were able to secure short-term instrumental cooperation with the peace process. Instrumental cooperation helped to reshape the Salvadoran political environment which altered identities and interests. Over time, self-sustaining norms supportive of human rights and pluralist, democracy were created.

Norms of democratic competition in El Salvador have taken root as the institutions and patterns of behavior shaped by strategic social construction have continued to develop in the absence of coercive aid. Commenting on El Salvador's dramatic transition, Orr writes,

Indeed, in the broader international context of peace efforts, El Salvador stands out for its successes. In 1999, seven years since signing peace accords, El Salvador has avoided a return to war, the human rights situation has dramatically improved, a variety of new institutions have been built, the economy has grown, and democracy is increasingly taking hold. In addition, the United Nations peace mission has pulled out and the United States has dramatically reduced its presence in the country, proving the country's internal capacity to sustain the peace process beyond an extensive, intrusive international presence.

(2001, 154)

El Salvador has continued to be rated as "Free" by Freedom House to 2003.[34] Despite this rating El Salvador is by no means a perfect society. While there was not full implementation of all of the provisions of the peace accords, there was substantial implementation which facilitated a significant political transition which has been sustained despite rising crime, a poor economy and the reappearance of "right-wing death squads, including 'social cleansing' vigilante groups." (Freedom House 2003) A decade after the departure of blue helmets, there has not been a large-scale return to political violence. By employing strategic social construction to support the development of new political norms, ONUSAL made a significant contribution to the durable, self-sustaining resolution of El Salvador's civil war.

Notes

1. The case history used in this chapter draws from the work of Hampson (1996a), Baranyi and North (1992; 1996), Johnstone (1995), Karl (1992), and Montgomery (1995a; 1995b). UN documents are reprinted in *The United Nations and El Salvador 1990-1995*, unless otherwise noted. It is important to note that while politically motivated violence has been greatly reduced with the end of El Salvador's civil war, violent crime has increased dramatically. For some Salvadorans insecurity has increased since the end of the conflict.

2. DOMREP (The Special Mission of the Secretary-General in the Dominican Republic; 1965-1966) consisted of three observers.

3. See A/44/344/Add.1-S/20699. Previous UN electoral experience had been limited to assistance in "non-self governing territory" such as Namibia as part of the UN's decolonization mandate (Lankevich 2001).

4. LeVine credits UN negotiators with persuading the FMLN to drop its demand for a transitional or coalition government and instead to focus on reform of existing political structures (1997, 236).

5. See Torres-Rivas' interview with FMLN leader Ana Guadalupe Martinez (1997).

6. Text of the Tela Declaration is reprinted in UN document A/44/451-S/20078.

7. Text of the Declaration of San Isidro de Coronado is reprinted in UN document A/44/872-S/21019.

8. Text reprinted in UN document A/45/706-S/21931, Annex II.

9. Text of the Caracas Agreement is reprinted in UN document A/48/706-S/21931, Annex II.

10. Armando Caldéron Sol represented ARENA in this forum. Caldéron Sol would become the first post-conflict president of El Salvador.

11. Text of the San José Agreement on Human Rights is reprinted in UN document A/44/971-S/21541.

12. Text of the Declaration of Puntarenas is reprinted in UN document A/45/906-S/22032.

13. Text of the Mexico Agreement reprinted in UN document A/46/553-S/23130.

14. Text of the New York Agreement is reprinted in UN document A/46/502-S/23082.

15. The New York Act I and New York Act II are reprinted in UN document A/46/863-S/23504.

16. Text of the Chapultepec Accords is reprinted in UN document A/46/864-S/23501.

17. See for example the objection of the Salvadoran government in UN document S/23999.

18. This provision reflects the fact that the Salvadoran government largely represented elites who "had accepted the need for economic liberalisation [but] had not accepted the need for redistribution" (Pearce 1999, 57). Also see Boyce (1995).

19. The Ad Hoc commission rested on "fragile legal ground" in Salvadoran law. Political realities undermined the commission's ability to comply with internationally recognized standards for evidence and due process which undermined the legitimacy of its findings in some eyes (Wilkins 1997, 265-266). Also see McCormick (1997, 293).

20. Reprinted in UN document S/25500.

21. Also see Spence and Vickers (1994).

22. Reprinted in *The United Nations and El Salvador: 1990-1995* (United Nations 1995a).

23. These caches included ground to air missiles (McCormick 1997, 287-287; Stanley and Holiday 1997, 31-32; Berdal 1993, 19). Many agree that the discovery of deception on the part of the FMLN was no real surprise as "most observers expected the FMLN to keep some weapons as a kind of guarantee" (Stanley and Holiday 1997, 31).

24. Also see (Stanley and Holiday (1997, 31-32) and Berdal (1993, 19).

25. FPL Secretary-General Sánchez Cerén as paraphrased by Boutros-Ghali wrote in his Report to the Security Council of 29 June 1993. Also see the original letter from Sánchez Cerén printed in UN document S/26005, Annex II (B).

26. FPL Secretary-General Sánchez Cerén as paraphrased by Boutros-Ghali wrote in his Report to the Security Council of 29 June 1993. Also see the original letter from Sánchez Cerén printed in UN document S/26005, Annex II (B).

27. Reprinted in UN document A/49/59-S/1994/47.

28. Rule of law, plural and representative democracy and reconciliation were also important themes in Calderon Sol's state of the nation address of 1 June 1995 (British Broadcasting Corporation 1995).

29. For example, the US donated 171 patrol cars valued at $2.3 million (United Press International 1994).

30. Not all demobilized soldiers were included in the program. Members of the *Asociación de Desmovilizzados de la Fuerza Armada de El Salvador* (ADEFAES), protesting non-receipt of benefits promised under the peace accords, occupied the Legislative Assembly, holding 15 legislatures and several hundred employees hostage for three days in January 1995. ONUSAL officers were able to temporarily defuse the protest, but demonstrations continued through 1995 as the government continued to ignore the organization's key demands (McCormick 1997; Williams and Walter 1997).

31. Reprinted in S/1994/1144, Annex.

32. Wendt's 'Three Degrees of Internalization' describes a similar process by which coercive, material and ideational forces combine to socially construct new intersubjective norms of legitimacy (1999). Also see Ruggie's concept of norm governed change (1983; 1998).

33. For more on the contradictory role played by international financial institutions see Boyce (1995) and Boyce and Pastor (1998).

34. Freedom House's *2003 Freedom in the World* lists El Salvador as "Free" from 1998 to 2003. During this period El Salvador received a score of 2 for political rights and 3 for civil liberties. From 1993 to 1997 El Salvador was rated as "Partly Free" scoring 3 in political rights and 3 in civil liberties.

Chapter 3

Cambodia

At the time it was created, the United Nations Transitional Authority in Cambodia (UNTAC) broke records as the largest and most expensive peace operation to be authorized by the UN Security Council. Fielding some 20,000 international civilian and military personnel at a cost of $1.6 billion, it was assigned the difficult task of implementing the 1991 Paris Peace Agreements. Despite the resources devoted to this operation, it was only a "qualified success" (Doyle and Suzuki 1995, 131) that helped to create "semipeace" (Doyle 2001). UNTAC did assist the repatriation of over 362,000 refugees and internally displaced persons, and organized Cambodia's first nationwide election. However, the demobilization provisions of the accords were abandoned after the Khmer Rouge withdrew from the peace process. For those parties that did participate in the electoral process, political violence and intimidation remained a regular feature of Cambodian life. Post-election political arrangements were the product of violence and intimidation "that erased many of the political gains made during and after" the UN operation. UNTAC left Cambodia "in almost the same condition as it was at the beginning of the decade, before the UN peace operation began" (Doyle 2001, 89).[1]

Unlike the Salvadoran peace process, international and regional supporters of the Paris Peace Agreements did not engage in a strategy of norm construction. Third-party supporters of the peace process did not articulate a consistent normative framework that might have guided the parties through negotiations and implementation and served as the foundation of post-conflict political life. Instead, challenges to implementation of the accords "were managed outside the guidelines ... of the UN-sponsored peace accords" (Munck and Kumar 1995, 165). Donors did not insist on full compliance with the terms of the accords as a condition of their aid. When implementation of the accords was challenged, donors accepted outcomes that were incompatible with the normative logic of the peace accords.

The Cambodia Problem

The civil war in Cambodia – the Cambodia or Kampuchea Problem as it was sometimes called – was shaped by internal power struggles, regional rivalries and the Cold War. Following the end of French colonization in 1955, Cambodia was ruled by Norodom Sihanouk.[2] In 1970, Sihanouk was overthrown in a coup by American-supported Lon Nol. Five years later Lon Nol was overthrown by the Chinese-supported Khmer Rouge. Under Pol Pot's leadership, the Khmer Rouge plunged the country into an "autogenocide" that led to the death of over one million Cambodians and triggered armed conflict with neighboring Vietnam. Vietnam invaded in late 1978 and installed Heng Samrin as head of the People's Republic of Kampuchea (PRK) on 8 January 1979.

Despite this tumultuous history, Cambodia received surprisingly little international attention in the 1970s. The Cambodian genocide was largely understood as a domestic matter and received little attention by the United Nations. Vietnam's invasion of Cambodia and the armed conflict that would continue through the next decade produced little official response from the UN Security Council. The Soviet Union supported the Vietnamese invasion and the government it established in Cambodia as the only humanitarian alternative to Pol Pot's Khmer Rouge. The Soviet Union and Vietnam provided economic and military support in the PRK's ongoing conflict with the Chinese-supported Khmer Rouge and Cambodia's other armed factions, Sihanouk's United National Front for an Independent, Neutral, Peaceful and Cooperative Cambodia (FUNCINPEC), and the smaller Khmer People's National Liberation Front (KPNLF) led by Sihanouk's former Prime Minister, Son Sann. FUNCINPEC and the KPNLF received support from the United States, the European Community, and the Association of South East Asian Nations (ASEAN). With its permanent members supporting competing groups, the threat of the veto precluded any real action by the Security Council.

Instead, the major arena for UN discussion of the conflict was the General Assembly. Here, most states were critical of Vietnam's *illegal* intervention and refused to extend formal recognition to the PRK government. As a result, the Khmer Rouge continued to represent Cambodia (Kampuchea) at the United Nations through 1981 when it joined with FUNCINPEC and the KPNLF to form the Coalition Government of Democratic Kampuchea (CGDK). The CGDK assumed the Cambodia seat in the General Assembly in 1982 (Prasad 2001). In the General Assembly, the ASEAN states — Indonesia, Thailand, Malaysia, the Philippines, Singapore and Brunei — spearheaded efforts to resolve the Cambodia problem as they understood it. The ASEAN states, particularly Vietnam's regional rival Thailand, were concerned with Vietnam's influence in the region. It is not surprising that ASEAN adopted the position that the Cambodia problem was a problem of Vietnam's illegal intervention in the internal affairs of Cambodia. The problem would be solved when Vietnam withdrew its forces and ended its support of the PRK. The domestic roots of conflict were largely ignored.

The ASEAN states sponsored UN General Assembly Resolution 34/22 which called for the withdrawal of "all foreign forces" and requested "all States to refrain from any interference in the internal affairs of Kampuchea in order to enable its people to decide their own future and destiny free from outside interference, subversion or coercion, and to respect scrupulously the sovereignty, territorial integrity, and independence of Kampuchea." The Secretary-General was asked to exercise his good offices to facilitate delivery of humanitarian aid as well as to find a peaceful solution. The resolution also called for an international conference on Kampuchea. The General Assembly approved the resolution on 14 November 1979 despite the protests of Vietnam and the Soviet bloc states.

The ASEAN states sponsored a second resolution the following year. It renewed the call for an international conference to "involve the participation of all conflicting parties in Kampuchea and others concerned" (A/RES/35/6). The resolution called for United Nations monitors to verify the withdrawal of foreign troops, monitor Cambodia's borders and supervise elections. The resolution also called for international assistance to ensure law and order and respect for human rights as well as international guarantees to ensure "Kampuchean independence, sovereignty, neutrality, and territorial integrity." It did not call for direct negotiations between Cambodia's armed factions. This resolution passed despite the protests of Vietnam and the Soviet Union. The International Conference on Kampuchea was held in New York in July 1981. Over 90 states were represented including Cambodia which was represented by the CGDK.

The PRK, Vietnam and the Soviet Union, however, continued to deny there was a Cambodia problem or at least one that was of international concern. In the words of the PRK foreign minister, "There is no Kampuchea problem and hence no solution for it." (quoted in Brown and Zasloff 1998). Without the participation of these key actors, it is not surprising that the conference had little immediate effect on the conflict itself.

Nonetheless, the conference's final statement, the "Declaration on Kampuchea," listed a number of principles which would serve as the basis of future peace initiatives. The "Declaration on Kampuchea" called for the withdrawal of foreign forces under UN supervision, a cease-fire, and respect for Kampuchea's independence and territorial integrity. It also called for "appropriate arrangements to ensure that armed Kampuchean factions are not able to prevent or disrupt the holding of free elections, or intimidate or coerce the population during the electoral process." (quoted in Brown and Zasloff 1998, 18) This basic formula for peace was reiterated in a series of ASEAN-sponsored resolutions that were passed annually by the General Assembly between 1979 and 1987 over the objections of Vietnam and the Soviet bloc.[3] All of these resolutions linked a "lasting peace in South-East Asia" with a comprehensive political settlement which included "the withdrawal of all foreign forces" and unspecified measures to "ensure respect for the sovereignty, independence, territorial integrity and neutral and non-aligned status of Kampuchea, as well as the right of the Kampuchean people to self-determination free from outside interference." (A/RES/42/3) Peace in Cambodia was equated with an end to foreign intervention. Cambodia's domestic political structure was not yet identified as part of the peace equation.

The Paris Peace Accords

As the Cold War came to an end in the late 1980s, there were a number of changes that enhanced the prospect of a negotiated settlement. Changing global geo-political relationships led the US, the Soviet Union and China to re-evaluate foreign policy, particularly foreign military and economic aid. All three states recognized that it was in their interest to bring an end to Cambodia's civil war. The potential for a negotiated settlement was also enhanced as the ASEAN states sought increasingly cooperative relations with Vietnam. As regional economic and security interests developed, it became increasingly important to Thailand, Indonesia, and other ASEAN states that Vietnam be more fully integrated with the rest of Southeast Asia. In addition to shifting global and regional geopolitical and economic interests, there were important changes in leadership in the Soviet Union, Vietnam and Cambodia. Upon being named as General Secretary of the Communist Party of the Soviet Union, Mikhail Gorbachev began a series of political and economic reforms. Soviet aid to Vietnam ended in 1985 triggering Vietnam's announcement that it would cut aid to the PRK and withdraw its forces from Cambodia by 1990 (Brown and Zasloff 1998).

Despite these changes, much more needed to be done before the conflict between the Cambodian parties themselves could be resolved. Although Hun Sen became Prime Minister of the PRK in 1985, the change in leadership did not mark an immediate change in the PRK's position that the Cambodia Problem was an internal matter to be resolved without foreign interference. In 1985 Malaysia's Foreign Minister proposed "Proximity Talks" in which all four Cambodian factions would participate in indirect, mediated talks. The proposal was rejected by the PRK and Vietnam on the grounds that such a meeting implied formal recognition of the Khmer Rouge (Prasad 2001). The issue of discussions involving all of the Cambodian factions was revisited later that year by Indonesia's Foreign Minister. In November Mochtar Kasumaatmadja discussed the idea of a "Cocktail Party" with Vietnamese diplomats. He argued the Cocktail Party format would allow all four of the Cambodian factions to participate, thus facilitating an end to the armed conflict, "without touching the undesirable question of recognition." (quoted in Prasad 2001, 83)

The first direct talks between Hun Sen, Prime Minister of the PRK, and Norodom Sihanouk, titular President of the CGDK and leader of FUNCINPEC, took place in Paris in December 1987. This meeting was followed by the first "Cocktail Party," (formally, the First Jakarta Informal Meeting (JIM I)) held in Bogor, Indonesia from 25-28 July 1988. This was the first time that all four Cambodian factions participated in face-to-face talks. Just days prior to this historic meeting, Hun Sen changed the official name of Cambodia from the People's Republic of Kampuchea (PRK) to the State of Cambodia (SOC), proclaimed Buddhism the national religion, and "abolished capital punishment as per the wishes of Prince Sihanouk" (Prasad 2001, 135). In this same period, Sihanouk resigned from the CGDK.

JIM I took place in two phases. First, the representatives of the four Cambodian factions attended meetings chaired by Indonesian Foreign Minister, Ali Alatas. Sihanouk did not participate directly but was in Jakarta as the private guest of President Suharto. This left FUNCINPEC to be represented by Sihanouk's son Prince Ranariddh. Son Sann represented the KPNLF; Khieu Samphan represented the Khmer Rouge; and Hun Sen represented the SOC. In the meeting's second phase, the Cambodians met with representatives of Vietnam, Laos, Indonesia, Thailand, Malaysia, the Philippines, Singapore and Brunei (Prasad 2001). The SOC and the CGDK each outlined their respective positions. While both sides agreed in principle to the withdrawal of Vietnamese forces, the end of foreign military assistance, and the establishment of a new government to be selected in a national election, there were also significant points of disagreement. The CGDK called for the creation of a four-party transitional government prior to elections as well as the integration of armed forces under a four-party joint command. The CGDK made no reference to an international peacekeeping force or third-party verification of the accords. In contrast, the SOC opposed Khmer Rouge participation in any interim government and insisted its own state apparatus continue to operate through the transition period. The SOC also opposed UN verification, but agreed to consider verification by either Canada or India (Brown and Zasloff 1998; Roberts 2001).

The Second Jakarta Informal Meeting (JIM II) took place from 19-21 February 1989 with the added participation of the United States, China and Japan. Following this round of talks, the Indonesian Foreign Ministry released a "Consensus Statement" which optimistically outlined the progress of the meeting:

- General acceptance of the need for a political settlement that would create "an independent, sovereign, peaceful, neutral, and non-aligned Kampuchea on the basis of self-determination and national reconciliation."

- Agreement to end all foreign interference in Cambodia. Withdrawal of Vietnamese forces would be linked to a cease-fire between the Cambodian factions to begin no later than 30 September 1989. Specific modalities would be determined in future negotiations.

- Agreement to prevent the recurrence of genocide and resumption of armed hostilities. Specific measures would be determined in future negotiations.

- Agreement that an International Control Mechanism (ICM) would be created to verify withdrawal of Vietnamese personnel and to prevent resumption of armed hostilities prior to elections. The composition and powers of the ICM would be determined in future negotiations.

- General elections would be held "in a free and democratic fashion" under ICM supervision.

- Internal affairs would be determined in private talks between the Cambodian factions.

- Once general consensus within the JIM process was reached, the parties agreed there would be a need for an international conference to guarantee full compliance, to secure international recognition of Cambodia's status as a "sovereign, independent, peaceful, neutral and non-aligned" state, to gain international support for reconstruction and development, and to fund the implementation process.[4]

Sihanouk vocally criticized the statement, claiming it reflected consensus "only between Indonesia, Vietnam and Hun Sen" (quoted in Prasad 2001, 135) and requested French President François Mitterand convene an international conference on Cambodia as an alternative venue for future negotiations. The Paris International Conference on Cambodia (PICC) was held from 30 July to 30 August 1989. Co-chaired by Roland Dumas, Foreign Minister of France and Ali Alatas, Foreign Minister of Indonesia, the conference was attended by the permanent members of the United Nations Security Council (China, France, the Soviet Union, the United States, and the United Kingdom), the ASEAN states (Brunei Darussalam, Malaysia, the Philippines, Singapore, Thailand, and Indonesia), Australia, Vietnam, Laos, Japan, India, Canada, and Zimbabwe (as Chairman of the Non-Aligned Movement). UN Secretary-General Javier Perez de Cuéllar and his Special Representative for Humanitarian Affairs in South-East Asia, Rafeeudin Ahmed, also attended as did Prince Sihanouk (representing FUNCINPEC), Son Sann (representing the KPNLF), Khieu Samphan (representing the Khmer Rouge), and Hun Sen (representing the SOC).

Old divisions continued to surface at the Paris Talks. Hun Sen criticized the international community for limiting its understanding of the conflict to "a problem between Vietnam and Cambodia, while keeping silent about the crimes of genocide of Pol Pot" (quoted in Lizée 2000, 56). In his view, the Khmer Rouge could not be allowed to return to power. The SOC opposed power sharing, particularly with the Khmer Rouge, and insisted that its administrative structures continue to operate (perhaps with monitoring by an international control mechanism) during the transition period.

Sihanouk, on the other hand, denied the existence of a civil war in Cambodia. He argued,

> what is known as the 'problem of Kampuchea' comprises, in reality, only one aspect that of the aggression (since 1978), military occupation, colonization, the Vietnamization of Cambodia... [the only conflict was] between Vietnam, the aggressor, and Cambodia, the aggressed party. (quoted in Lizée 2000, 57)

This position was supported in statements to the Conference by Khieu Samphan and Son Sann (Lizée 2000). The CGDK argued that a power sharing government must be created prior to elections and that the Khmer Rouge could not be excluded. It also sought to limit the influence of the SOC during the transition period through extensive international monitoring and control of SOC administrative bodies.

Despite continuing disagreement, the Paris Talks did produce general understanding on a number of issues. An international control mechanism would be created to oversee implementation of a comprehensive peace settlement, including military and electoral provisions of the accords. Agreements in principle were also made on the issues of repatriation of refugees and internally displaced persons, and reconstruction. Unlike the Salvadoran peace process, these tentative points of agreement were not formalized by signed, written agreements due to the P5's preference for a comprehensive agreement (Roberts 2001; Munck and Kumar 1995).

By the end of September 1989, Vietnamese forces were completely withdrawn from Cambodia: ahead of schedule, without international verification and without a peace agreement between the Cambodian parties. The Vietnamese withdrawal had little effect on Cambodia's internal balance of power; the military stalemate between the CGDK (dominated militarily by the Khmer Rouge) and the SOC continued. Stalemate, however, was not enough to trigger a significant change in bargaining positions. While both sides accepted elections in theory, significant disagreement remained. The CGDK insisted the four Cambodian factions participate in a powersharing government prior to elections. The SOC refused "on grounds that it would return the Khmer Rouge to power" (Gottesman 2003, 336-7). The parties also disagreed on military and security issues as well as the role of international monitors.

While the Cambodians continued the military and political stalemate, the P5 worked to develop a plan for peace based on the late-1989 proposal by Australian Foreign Minister, Gareth Evans. Key to Evans' proposal was the suggestion that the United Nations participate in Cambodia's transitional administration (Evans 1994). Evans' suggestion was "not rejected" by the Cambodian parties and "quickly embraced" by the international community (Gottesman 2003, 337). Meeting in Paris in January 1990, the P5 reached tentative agreement on the outline of a peace plan. Its first assumption was that "[n]o acceptable solution can be achieved by force of arms." The plan envisioned an active UN role in both the negotiation and implementation phases of the peace process. The UN would be asked to verify the withdrawal of foreign forces, cessation of foreign military aid, and a cease-fire. The UN would also ensure internal security during the transition period and administer elections "conducted in a neutral political environment in which no party would be advantaged... All Cambodians should enjoy the same rights, freedoms, and opportunities to participate in the election process." (S/21087) The P5 welcomed regional efforts "to achieve a comprehensive political settlement ... with a view to reconvening the Paris Conference at an appropriate time." (S/21087)

The ASEAN states, particularly Thailand and Indonesia, also remained actively engaged in the Cambodian peace process. As Japan came to believe that it would be asked to make a significant financial contribution to the costs of peacebuilding and postwar reconstruction, it also became an active participant (Chanda 1990). In early 1990 Japan's Foreign Ministry, with the support of Thai Prime Minister Chatichai, reintroduced the peace proposal first discussed by Sihanouk and Hun Sen in 1989. Unlike the P5 plan, it envisioned a settlement that would exclude the Khmer Rouge from future Cambodian governments and limit the UN's role in elections (Brown and Zasloff 1998; Roberts 2001). Though this initiative was soon tabled after the Khmer Rouge walked out of talks in Tokyo (Chanda 1990), it marked the beginning of what would become a pattern of inconsistent norm articulation. Whereas the P5 proposal ensured the participation of all four Cambodian factions and asserted a substantial UN role in monitoring and administrating the transition process, the Asian initiative proposed a limited international role in a transition that would exclude the Khmer Rouge from post-conflict institutions.

While the Asian approach stalled, the P5 continued its efforts and released the Framework Document in late-August. The key provisions of the Framework Document include:

- United Nations Transitional Authority in Cambodia (UNTAC) — UNTAC was to supervise and monitor implementation of the peace accords from the time of signature of the final treaty to the adoption of a new Cambodian constitution. UNTAC would ensure that elections for a Constituent Assembly took place in a neutral political environment and would "supervise and control" agencies "that could directly influence the outcome of elections" particularly foreign affairs, national defense, finance, public security and information.

- Supreme National Council (SNC) — The Supreme National Council would be composed of "representative individuals ... committed to the holding of free and fair elections as the basis for forming a new and legitimate government." Membership would be determined by the Cambodian parties but "no party should be dominant in this process." Election of Sihanouk as SNC President would be "welcome." The SNC would delegate to UNTAC "all powers necessary to ensure the implementation of the comprehensive agreement." With the consensus of its members, the SNC was to offer UNTAC advice. The Special Representative of the Secretary-General could determine whether or not the SNC's advice was consistent with the comprehensive political settlement.

- Demobilization — UNTAC would supervise, monitor and verify the cease-fire including the withdrawal of all foreign forces, advisors, military personnel and equipment following a cease-fire. "All forces" would participate in regroupment, cantonment, and arms reduction under UNTAC supervision.

- Elections — UNTAC would monitor and supervise elections for a National Assembly. The National Assembly would write Cambodia's new constitution.

- Human Rights — Relevant international human rights instruments would be adopted to "ensure the non-return to the policies and practices of the past" (i.e., genocide).[5]

Curiously, the Cambodian factions did not participate in the negotiations that created the Framework Document. It was only after the fact that France and Indonesia, as PICC co-chairs, sought to persuade the four Cambodian parties of the proposal's merit. Following their meeting in Jakarta on 9-10 September 1990, the first joint statement of all four Cambodian factions was issued.[6] They agreed to accept the P5 Framework Document "in its entirety" and to create the Supreme National Council (SNC) as the "unique legitimate body and source of authority in which, throughout the transitional period, the independence, sovereignty and unity of Cambodia is embodied." The SNC would delegate to the UN "all powers necessary to ensure the implementation of the comprehensive agreement, including those relating to the conduct of free and fair elections and the relevant aspects of the administration of Cambodia" (A/45/490-S/21732, Annex).

Despite apparent acceptance of the Framework Document by all four Cambodian factions, the peace process remained stalled for the next several months as the Cambodians struggled to reach agreement on the SNC. Following the Jakarta meeting, the Cambodian parties announced the SNC would be made up of twelve "individuals with authority among the Cambodian people and reflecting all shades of opinion among them" which would make decisions "by consensus" (Prasad 2001, 150). This formulation allowed each of the Cambodian parties to participate in the SNC without granting each other formal recognition. Informally, it was agreed that the SOC would control six seats while FUNCINPEC, the KPNLF and the Khmer Rouge would each control two. Sihanouk would chair the SNC as its thirteenth member (Prasad 2001, 150). However, when representatives of the four Cambodian factions met on 17 September 1990, the SOC delegates refused to name Sihanouk SNC Chairman unless Hun Sen was named Vice-Chairman and selected to head Cambodia's delegation to the United Nations. The meeting ended without agreement.

The Framework Document was formally endorsed by the Security Council in Resolution 668 on 20 September 1990 and by acclamation of the General Assembly on 15 October. Resolution 668 also called upon France and Indonesia to reconvene the Paris International Conference on Cambodia (PICC). The Paris Conference, however, was not reconvened until the SNC was formed. In the meantime, the P5 reaffirmed its preference that Sihanouk be named SNC chairman but agreed to defer to the Cambodian parties on specific issues of size, membership and leadership, including whether or not the SNC was to have a vice-chair. The P5, however, was unwilling to let the dispute stand in the way of the peace process. In cooperation with the Secretary-General's Special Representative and the PICC Co-chairs, the P5 issued the "Proposed structure for the agreements on a comprehensive political settlement of the Cambodia conflict," (the Draft Agreement) on 26 November 1990.[7] The Draft Agreement built on the Framework Document adding details about elections, the constitution, refugees and internally displaced persons, and rehabilitation and reconstruction. Its main provisions include:

- Supreme National Council (SNC) — The SNC was to offer "advice" to the Special Representative of the Secretary-General (SRSG) on a consensus basis. The SRSG was to determine whether or not the SNC's advice was consistent with the comprehensive political settlement. If the SNC could not reach consensus, the SRSG was to have final decision making authority.

- Demobilization — The Draft Agreement affirmed the Framework Documents plan for international supervision of cantonment of "all forces" and outlined a two-phase plan for disarmament and demobilization. In the first phase, each Cambodian faction was to maintain custody of its own weapons. The second phase would begin after cantonment of all forces was verified by UNTAC. During this phase, custody of all military equipment would be transferred to UNTAC. Final disposition of weapons would be determined by Cambodia's post-election government. UNTAC was authorized to investigate violations brought to its attention by the parties or on its own initiative.

- Elections — The Draft Agreement defined eligible voters as all persons born in Cambodia or the child of a person born in Cambodia at least 18 years old during the registration period. Procedures for the registration of political parties were also described. While the Draft Agreement did not specify the size of the Constituent Assembly, representatives were to be elected by "a system of proportional representation on the basis of lists of candidates put forward by political parties." UNTAC was to supervise and control administrative agencies that might "directly influence the outcome of elections."

- Constituent Assembly — The Constituent Assembly was to draft a new Cambodian constitution within three months of its establishment. Cambodia's new constitution was to respect the rule of law under a political system that included "periodic and genuine elections," and an independent judiciary. Cambodia's new constitution was to enshrine human rights "consistent with the provisions of the Universal Declaration of Human Rights and other international instruments." Once the new constitution was adopted, the Constituent Assembly would convert itself to Cambodia's first Legislative Assembly.

- Refugees and Internally Displaced Persons (IDPs) — UNHCR was designated the lead agency in this area.

The "Declaration on the Rehabilitation and Reconstruction of Cambodia" was released at the same time as the Draft Agreement. It identified Cambodia's need for both short and long-term assistance and asserted the principle that the post-election government would determine Cambodia's development needs.

Representatives of the four Cambodian factions met in Paris with PICC co-chairs and the Secretary-General' Special Representative in late December 1990. In a statement issued following this meeting, the Cambodians accepted the Draft Agreement "on most of the fundamental points." An additional "Explanatory Note," was dedicated to clarifying UNTAC's role in the transition process. UNTAC would conduct "guidance and surveillance" activities and "control" key administrative areas including information, finance, public security, national defense and foreign affairs to ensure elections took place in a neutral political environment. In consultation with the SNC, UNTAC would also "exercise control" or "supervise" additional administrative bodies that might directly influence the outcome of the election and investigate complaints (but not "control" or "supervise") state administrative activities necessary to the normal day-to-day life of Cambodians. The statement specified:

> The interaction (control, supervise, investigation) will be limited to those functions and activities of the existing administrative structures, [...] which could directly influence the holding of free and fair elections in a neutral political environment. *Other functions and activities will remain unaffected.*
> (A/46/61-S/22059, emphasis added)

While the "Explanatory Note" expressed the common position of the Cambodian factions with respect to UNTAC, significant disagreement remained. The CGDK accepted provision of the Draft Agreement that required complete demobilization and disarmament prior to elections. Citing security concerns, the SOC objected. Additionally, the SOC insisted the peace accords include explicit references to the Khmer Rouge's history of genocide. This provision was unacceptable to the Khmer Rouge and rejected by the CGDK (Davidson 1990).

While the P5 continued to insist upon a comprehensive settlement, regional actors, particularly Thailand and Japan, advocated an incremental process

(Heininger 1994). In February 1991 Japan presented its own proposal. Seeking to address SOC's security concerns, it called for UN verification of each stage of the demobilization process. Violators would not be allowed to participate in elections. The Japanese plan also sought to address the SOC's demand that the peace agreement include formal recognition of the Khmer Rouge's genocidal history. The Japanese proposed a the creation of a committee to be composed of the four Cambodian factions, UNTAC and the United Nations High Commissioner on Refugees which would investigate the Khmer Rouge's human rights record from 1975 to 1979 (Takeda 1998; Kiernan 1993a). As with its previous diplomatic initiative, the Khmer Rouge (with China's support) rejected the Japanese proposal.

The June meeting between the Cambodian factions in Jakarta did little to advance the peace process. Progress was made when the SNC, representatives from France and Indonesia, and the Special Representative of the Secretary-General, met in Pattaya, Thailand, in late June 1991. This meeting produced a number of agreements between the parties including: selection of a flag and anthem for the SNC; agreement to establish SNC headquarters in Phnom Penh; and agreement on security arrangements for SNC residences in Phnom Penh. States were invited to establish diplomatic relations with the SNC and to open embassies in Phnom Penh for this purpose. Future meetings of the SNC and its working groups were to discuss the rules and procedures of the SNC, principles of the new constitution, and electoral laws (A/45/271-S/22740). Most significantly, it was agreed that Sihanouk would have the authority to convene the SNC although formally the issue of SNC membership and leadership remained unresolved. The Cambodian factions also agreed to stop arms imports and began an "indefinite ceasefire" (Financial Times 1991).

In the absence of a disengagement plan or monitoring, the first Cambodian cease-fire soon broke down. A second cease-fire was announced in July 1991. That same month, Cambodian representatives met in Beijing where the outstanding issues of SNC leadership and membership were finally resolved. Following his agreement to resign from his other political positions, Sihanouk was named SNC President. Under the leadership of a "neutral" Sihanouk, the SNC was comprised of eleven additional members; six named by the SOC and five by the CGDK.

With the SNC formally constituted, the Cambodians met with representatives of the P5 and SRSG Ahmed in Pattaya in late August 1991 to discuss the Draft Agreement. The SNC seemed most unified in their attempt to limit the authority of the SRSG. Where the Draft Agreement authorized the SRSG to make final decisions if the SNC was unable to reach consensus, the SNC proposed Sihanouk be allowed to speak on its behalf in the absence of unanimity. This change was not accepted by the P5. While the Cambodians confirmed their intention to "adopt a system of liberal, multiparty democracy" and to "encourage respect for the observance of human rights and fundamental freedoms" (A/14/418-S/23011) as described in the Draft Agreement, there was little agreement on how the legislative body would be formed. Not surprisingly, the

CGDK delegates accepted the system of proportional representation outlined in the Draft Agreement. Such a system could be expected to provide it maximal representation. The SOC, however, already firmly in power in most of Cambodia argued in favor of a single ballot constituency system. This system was expected to minimize CGDK influence (Agence France Presse 1991e). A compromise of proportional representation at the provincial level was suggested by SRSG Ahmed and was accepted by all four Cambodian factions and the P5 in the New York meeting the following month (Ratner 1993a; Heininger 1994).

Despite positive movement in some areas, the Pattaya meeting revealed the SOC's continued distrust of the Khmer Rouge. The SOC objected to the Draft Agreement's plan for complete disarmament and demobilization prior to elections. It argued that because its forces were easier to monitor, the disarmament provisions of the Draft Agreement would leave it effectively disarmed while the Khmer Rouge, hiding in the jungle, would be able to retain much of its military capacity. Hun Sen was particularly concerned that this would leave the SOC vulnerable to a Khmer Rouge attack (Heininger 1994).[8] This prompted adoption of the 70-30 plan suggested by French diplomat Jean-David Levitte. 70 percent of forces were to be demobilized and disarmed prior to elections. The remaining 30 percent were to be cantoned during elections. The post-election government would then be able to choose complete demobilization or incorporation under a new military structure (Agence France Presse 1991c; 1991e). Though accepted by the members of the SNC, this compromise was only reluctantly accepted by the P5 which continued to argue in favor of complete demobilization prior to elections (Heininger 1994; Brown and Zasloff 1998).

The SOC also continued to push for inclusion of language that would explicitly put responsibility for the Cambodian genocide on the Khmer Rouge and provide guarantees that it would not be allowed to return to power (Financial Times 1991). While the Khmer Rouge officially objected to any reference to genocide in the final peace accords, there were media reports of an informal agreement that those most closely identified with the genocide would not formally participate in the new government. Agence France Presse reported, "Pol Pot and other senior Khmer Rouge leaders responsible for atrocities during their rule... would not be a candidate although they will not give up political work completely as they intend to 'encourage' the Khmer Rouge in the U.N.-organised poll." (Birsel 1991)

Negotiations between the SNC and the P5 continued in New York in September. In addition to formally accepting Ahmed's compromise on the electoral system, the relationship between the SRSG and the SNC was resolved. The SRSG was to have final decision making authority if the President of the SNC was unable or unwilling to make a decision on behalf of the SNC. With agreement on these key issues the Paris International Conference for Cambodia was scheduled to reconvene in October (Agence France Presse 1991d). In anticipation of the final accords, the Security Council approved the creation of The United Nations Advance Mission in Cambodia (UNAMIC) on 16 October 1991.

The Paris Peace Accords — The Agreement on a Comprehensive Settlement of the Cambodia Conflict, the Agreement Concerning the Sovereignty, Independence and Territorial Integrity and Inviolability, Neutrality and National Unity of Cambodia, and the Declaration on the Rehabilitation and Reconstruction of Cambodia — were signed by the 19 state participants of the Paris International Conference for Cambodia on 23 October 1991. The key provisions of the accords were:

- United Nations Transitional Authority in Cambodia (UNTAC) — UNTAC was to ensure a neutral political environment during the transitional period. It was granted the authority to engage in "supervision or control" of the "administrative agencies, bodies and offices which could directly influence the outcome of elections." The transitional period was to begin the day the Paris Peace Agreements were signed and end three months following the formation of the Constituent Assembly.

- Supreme National Council (SNC) — The SNC would serve as the "unique legitimate body and source of authority in which, through the transitional period, the sovereignty, independence and unity of Cambodia are enshrined." The SNC would in turn delegate "all powers necessary to ensure the implementation of this Agreement" to UNTAC.

- Constituent Assembly — A 120-seat Constituent Assembly would be selected in UN-sponsored elections. The Assembly was to draft a new constitution consistent with "a system of liberal democracy" that would respect pluralism, human rights and fundamental freedoms. With at least a two-thirds majority of the Constituent Assembly, the new constitution was to be adopted within three months of its inauguration.

- Disarmament and Demobilization — UNTAC's military division was to verify withdrawal of foreign forces, monitor the cease-fire, and verify the cantonment of Cambodian forces during the transition period. At least 70 percent of each faction's forces were to be demobilized prior to voter registration. The remaining 30 percent of forces would be cantoned during the transition period and were to be either demobilized following elections or reorganized under the direction of the new Cambodian government. Weapons of cantoned forces would be stored under UNTAC control. UNTAC was also authorized to monitor the cessation of outside military assistance to the Cambodian parties from checkpoints within Cambodia. UNTAC was authorized to investigate violations on its own initiative at any time and to investigate violations brought to its attention by the Cambodian parties during the second phase of the disarmament and demobilization process.

- Law and Order — UNTAC's civilian police division (CIVPOL) was to ensure law and order, and impartial respect for human rights during the transition period. CIVPOL was authorized to supervise Cambodia's law enforcement and judicial system. Each faction was to provide UNTAC with information about the size, location and armaments of its police forces.

- Rehabilitation and Reconstruction — The Secretary-General was asked to appoint a representative to coordinate short-term rehabilitation aid. Planning for long-term development assistance was to take place after the transition period. The post-election government was designated with "primary responsibility for determining Cambodia's reconstruction needs ... foreigners should not impose a development strategy upon the country."

- Repatriation of Refugees and Internally Displaced Persons — UNHCR as the designated lead agency was to coordinate efforts to ensure full repatriation of refugees and internally displaced persons prior to elections.[9]

With the Paris Peace Agreements signed, the way was cleared for the formal creation and deployment of the United Nations Advance Mission in Cambodia (UNAMIC). Fifty military liaison officers arrived in Cambodia on 9 November 1991 with the primary mission of helping to maintain the fragile ceasefire (Boutros-Ghali 1995c). They established Mixed Military Working Groups (MMWGs) that helped to improve communication between the factions and facilitated disengagement of forces and deployment of UN military observers (Babb and Steuber 1998; Lizée 2000). UNAMIC also included a 20-person mine awareness unit that worked in conjunction with UNHCR's mine-clearing programme that trained civilians to avoid land mines and booby-traps as well as to clear mines and repair roads and bridges. The Security Council Authorized an additional 1,000 soldiers to aid mine clearance efforts in early January 1992 (S/RES/728).

Most observers argued that peace in Cambodia would be greatly aided by the swift and complete deployment of UNTAC. Planning for the United Nations Transitional Authority began soon after the Paris Agreements were signed. Between October and December 1991, three survey missions were dispatched to assess mission needs for elections, demobilization, civil administration, civilian police, and human rights (S/23613). Yasushi Akashi, a career UN official from Japan, was named to be the Secretary-General's Special Representative for Cambodia on 9 January. In an effort to expedite deployment, the Secretary-General asked the General Assembly to authorize the first tranche of UNTAC funding prior to Security Council approval of the implementation plan. The General Assembly approved an initial allocation of $200 million on 14 February 1992.

The Secretary-General's plan for implementation was submitted to the Security Council on 19 February 1992. It called for a complex peacebuilding operation to be composed of seven operational components: human rights, electoral, military, civil administration, police, repatriation, and rehabilitation.

Boutros-Ghali outlined the objectives of each division as agreed to in the Paris Agreements as well as an implementation timetable. The implementation plan called for full deployment of the military component by the end of May 1992 with demobilization of 70 percent of forces expected by the end of September after which the UNTAC military component was to be reduced as Cambodian forces demobilized. A three-month voter registration period was to begin in October. Elections were scheduled to take place in April or May both because of the significant additional costs expected should elections be held during the rainy season and also because this timeframe corresponded to the Cambodian New Year, a period in which most Cambodians traditionally return to their home district. Under the terms of the Paris Agreement, UNTAC was to withdraw at the end of the transitional period defined as three months following the establishment of the Constituent Assembly (S/23613). A projected budget soon followed. UNTAC was expected to cost $1.9 billion dollars plus resettlement costs for 360,000 refugees and internally displaced persons (S/23613, Addendum).

UNTAC was formally created on 28 February 1992 following the Security Council's approval of the Secretary-General's plan for implementation. The authorizing resolution confirmed Boutros-Ghali's recommended timetable with elections to be held by May 1993 "at the latest." UNTAC was to remain in Cambodia "for a period not to exceed eighteen months." (S/RES/745) With an approved mandate and initial funding, the task of finding qualified personnel began in earnest. Not only did UNTAC compete for resources and personnel with the newly established UN operation in Yugoslavia, the Cambodian mission faced the added difficulty of finding staff with appropriate administrative and linguistic skills. Very few non-Cambodians spoke Khmer. As a legacy of the Pol Pot period and the country's relative isolation under the PRK, French and English were not widely spoken inside Cambodia. The initial deployment of UNTAC personnel, including SGSR Akashi and UNTAC Force Commander, Australian Lieutenant-General John Sanderson did not take place until 15 March 1992 at which time UNAMIC was folded into UNTAC's military component (S/23870). As UNTAC deployed, it was clear that peacebuilding in Cambodia would not be easy. Eighty-percent of Cambodian territory was ruled by the SOC as a one-party state. The rest of Cambodia was controlled by either the Khmer Rouge, the KPNLF, or FUNCINPEC. Each group controlled its territory to the exclusion of the others. Peacebuilders would need to both reduce armed violence in Cambodian society as well as build democratic political norms if peacebuilding was going to have lasting effects.

Implementation

As UNTAC prepared to deploy, violations of the cease-fire became an increasingly frequent occurrence despite calls from the Secretary-General, the Security Council and others that the party's observe the terms of the Paris Agreements.

Large-scale fighting between the SOC and Khmer Rouge broke out in January 1992 (Babb and Steuber 1998; Lizée 2000). In addition, the Khmer Rouge refused UN personnel full access to territory under its control and a UN helicopter was targeted by small arms fire in late February. A subsequent UN enquiry identified the Khmer Rouge as the responsible party, an accusation they denied (S/23870).

It was not until March 1992 that UNTAC began to establish itself as an operational presence in Cambodia. With the help of personnel initially deployed under UNAMIC, UNTAC worked to re-establish the cease-fire and secure implementation of other provisions of the accords. In addition, preparations for refugee repatriation, elections and supervision of civilian police and administrative structures also began. In addition to cease-fire violations, UNTAC worked to improve human rights, particularly political freedom. Shortly after arriving in country, Akashi expressed concern that local authorities did not treat politically motivated attacks as "an important priority" (S/23870, para. 11). Although the SOC publicly announced its commitment to liberal democracy based on the principles of separation of powers, pluralism, and respect for human rights in late 1991, Cambodia's political environment was largely unchanged (Gottesman 2003). Privately, the SOC issued directives forbidding Cambodians from speaking to foreigners and temporarily closed the universities, thus bringing "an end to Cambodia's brief experiment in free expression." (Sanger 1991) Similarly, the SNC announced agreement on rules for the formation of political parties and independent newspapers at the end of 1991 (Agence France Presse 1992e). However, in practice the Cambodian parties used violence and intimidation to prevent political competitors from operating in territory under their control. Officially Cambodia promised "democratic freedoms but subjected those who exercised them to threats and violence." (Gottesman 2003, 348)[10] Akashi's demand that local authorities treat politically motivated attacks as "an important priority" (S/23870, para. 11) met with little immediate change in practice.

In April, the Secretary-General visited Phnom Penh and launched $593 million international appeal for Cambodia's rehabilitation. The Secretary-General's visit allowed him to witness the SNC accede to the International Covenant on Civil and Political Rights and the International Covenant on Economic, Social and Cultural Rights (Heininger 1994).[11] Aware of the problems associated with the exercise of political and civil rights in Cambodia, Boutros-Ghali urged the Cambodians "take necessary measures to ensure that the principles contained in the Covenants are applied in a concrete manner." (S/23870, para. 14)

The Secretary-General's report of 1 May 1992 reflected UNTAC's mixed experience in Cambodia. On a positive note, preparations for elections were underway and 526 men, women and children had been successfully relocated in a test of the repatriation program. Continued progress in both areas was expected. While relations between UNTAC and the SNC were described as "constructive" (S/23870, para. 4), the report expressed concern both that UNTAC personnel did not enjoy freedom of movement in Khmer Rouge-controlled territory and that the cease-fire had not been fully restored. The report also noted with concern ongoing politically motivated attacks and human rights violations (S/23870).

Despite cease-fire violations and ongoing political violence and intimidation, UN officials were sufficiently optimistic to announce plans for phase II of the cease-fire in early May. After consulting the four Cambodian factions and receiving their assurance that UNTAC personnel would be granted freedom of movement, Sanderson announced regroupment and cantonment of armed forces would begin on 13 June 1992. In preparation for phase II, the four Cambodian factions also promised to mark minefields and agreed to provide UNTAC with information about troops, arms and equipment. The Khmer Rouge, however, continued to interfere with the movements of UNTAC's military component. It also failed to mark minefields in territory under its control and did not provide data as promised (S/24090).

Akashi raised the issue of Khmer Rouge non-compliance at the SNC meeting of 26 May 1992. He also outlined a number of steps the Khmer Rouge must take to demonstrate its willingness to enter the second phase of demobilization. Among other measures, he demanded the cease-fire be respected and that UNTAC be allowed to exercise unrestricted freedom of movement as required by the Paris Accords. He also called on the Khmer Rouge to mark mine fields in territory under its control and provide UNTAC with data on troops and arms as previously agreed. Akashi also demanded that the Khmer Rouge "refrain from including in their radio broadcasts misinformation about UNTAC activities and intentions" (S/24090, para. 3). Days later, Akashi and Sanderson were prevented from entering Khmer Rouge-held territory near Pailin. Though Akashi brought the incident to the attention of the SNC and reported the Khmer Rouge's violations to UN headquarters, his efforts produced little more than admonishments to the parties to fulfill their obligations under the Paris Accords.

The Khmer Rouge did not alter its behavior and instead responded with charges that UNTAC had failed to fulfill its responsibilities under the accords. It complained that UNTAC had never sufficiently verified the withdrawal and non-return of Vietnamese personnel and insisted that foreign personnel remained in Cambodia in violation of the Paris Agreements. The Khmer Rouge was also very critical of what it termed the inability or unwillingness of UNTAC to exercise control over the SOC's administrative bodies and called on the SNC to play a more prominent role during the transition period. The Khmer Rouge was not alone in this complaint. Sihanouk spent much of the transition period out of the country where he repeatedly denounced UNTAC for not asserting more control over SOC authorities. The KPNLF and FUNCINPEC were also critical of UNTAC's supervision of the SOC's administration but, unlike the Khmer Rouge, did not make supervision to their satisfaction a condition for continued cooperation with the implementation process (Peou 2000).

In early June, the Khmer Rouge announced it would not participate in the second phase of demobilization unless UNTAC agreed to verify the withdrawal of *all* Vietnamese troops and the SOC agreed to effectively surrender power to the SNC (Agence France Presse 1992d). In mid-June, Khieu Samphan made two additional demands: 1) ethnic-Vietnamese must be excluded from participating in elections (a demand already made by the KPNLF); and 2) the SOC must not be allowed to control disbursement of foreign aid (Agence France Presse 1992d). Although, the Khmer Rouge spoke of its commitment to full implementation of the Paris Peace Accords in its correspondence with UN officials (United Nations 1995c), its demands threatened to unravel the peace process.

As efforts to persuade the Khmer Rouge to cooperate more fully with UNTAC continued, Sanderson and Boutros-Ghali argued that demobilization should continue despite the Khmer Rouge. Postponement would likely lead to delayed implementation of other aspects of the accords and push elections beyond the May 1993 target date.[12] As the June 13 approached, it was recognized that the non-participation of the Khmer Rouge would require adjustments in the demobilization plan (S/24090). Efforts to convince the Khmer Rouge to enter the second phase of demobilization were to continue as the KPNLF, FUNCINPEC and the SOC prepared to participate in a scaled-down demobilization program.

The Tokyo Ministerial Conference on Rehabilitation and Reconstruction of Cambodia was held on 20 and 22 June 1992. With most of the signators of the peace accords present, it provided a good opportunity to discuss the implementation process and the crisis triggered by the Khmer Rouge's announcement that it would not participate in the demobilization process. On 22 June representatives of the P5, the co-chairs of PICC, and the SRSG presented a non-paper, "A Proposal for Discussion" to the four Cambodian parties. It outlined talking points designed to improve cooperation between UNTAC and the Cambodian factions including suggestions for active cooperation in the verification of the withdrawal and non-return of foreign personnel. It also proposed ways in which consultations between UNTAC and the SNC could be enhanced, including increased consultations on the sensitive issues of visa distribution, foreign trade, and foreign investment. The non-paper clarified that financial and other support was understood to apply to all of Cambodian territory, according to need, and acknowledged the need. While the "Proposal for Discussion" was accepted by the SOC, FUNCINPEC and the KPNLF, the Khmer Rouge "did not reject the proposal, but promised to consider it and make known its views at a later stage." (S/24286, para. 7)

At least some of the conference participants considered economic sanctions against the Khmer Rouge. Despite the end of Chinese aid, the Khmer Rouge was able to continue its campaign of violence at least in part because it controlled valuable gem and timber resources along the Thai-Cambodian border. The Khmer Rouge, working with companies tied to elements of the Thai military and political elite, exported these resources and imported military equipment and other supplies. Sanctions, therefore, would not be effective without Thai support (Agence France Presse 1992a). However, Thailand's Foreign Minister, Arsa Sarasin, cautioned conference participants "not to expect too much from his country" and warned against "excessively high expectations in Thailand's ability in advancing the peace process." (Sarasin quoted in Agence France Presse 1992c)

The delegates to the Tokyo Conference stopped short of adopting a strategy of strategic social construction; Economic sanctions and aid conditionality would not be used to support implementation of the Paris Accords. Two formal statements were released at the conference's conclusion. "The Tokyo Declaration on the Cambodia Peace Process"[13] called on all parties to comply with the terms of the Paris Accords in a timely fashion so that elections could take place as scheduled. Referring to the Khmer Rouge, the statement called on "the party to cooperate with UNTAC in the full and timely implementation of the second phase of the cease-fire and to meet promptly its obligations under the Agreements" (A/47/285-S/24183, Annex I). The Declaration also called for the full deployment of UNTAC's military and civilian components and stressed "the need for UNTAC to exercise its mandate ... to ensure a neutral political environment." (A/47/285-S/24183, Annex I, para. 6). There was no mention of specific measures that might be taken against those who failed to cooperate with UNTAC or fulfill their obligations under the Paris Accords. "The Tokyo Declaration on the Rehabilitation and Reconstruction of Cambodia"[14] affirmed that rehabilitation and reconstruction aid "should be made available impartially, with full regard to Cambodia's sovereignty, benefit all regions of Cambodia and reach all levels of society and the most needy sectors of the population." (A/47/285-S/24183, Annex II) In the language of the Paris Agreements, this seemed to identify a significant role for the SNC as the embodiment of Cambodia's sovereignty during the transition period and asserted a principle of aid distribution at odds with the principle of aid conditionality that would have allowed aid to be allocated to reward compliance with the Paris Accords.[15]

As efforts to secure Khmer Rouge cooperation proceeded, it continued to make its own demands. While repeatedly refusing to express an opinion on the non-paper, it issued its own proposals, including restrictions on the SOC beyond the provisions of the Paris Accords (United Nations 1995c). In his second special report on UNTAC of 14 July 1992, the Secretary-General identified a number of steps that had been taken to address the Khmer Rouge's concerns with the implementation process. In addition to adding border checkpoints along the Vietnamese-Cambodian border, UNTAC deployed mobile teams to verify the non-return of Vietnamese military personnel. All of the Cambodian parties were invited to participate in the verification process. UNTAC also clarified the term foreign personnel as defined by the accords and refused to adopt the Khmer Rouge's position that former members of the Vietnamese military who had settled in Cambodia (often with Cambodian wives and children) be included in this category (Jordens 1996; Heininger 1994). UNTAC also sought to increase recruitment of civilian administrative staff and was considering the creation of "working groups" to improve communication between UNTAC and the SNC in the areas of foreign affairs, national defense, finance, public security and information. The Secretary-General, however, noted that the Khmer Rouge's demand with respect to the SOC administrative structures violated the terms of the Paris Accords and could not be entertained (S/24286).

While diplomats continued talks with the Khmer Rouge, the Security Council introduced the principle of aid conditionality, requesting that the Secretary-General and his Special Representative

> ensure that international assistance to the rehabilitation and reconstruction of Cambodia from now on benefits only the parties which are fulfilling their obligations under the Paris agreements and cooperating fully with the Authority.
>
> (S/RES/766, para. 12)

While officially the Security Council made implementation of the Paris Accords a condition for aid the, some doubted that Resolution 766 would have a real impact on the situation given the Khmer Rouge's control of valuable natural resources along the porous Thai-Cambodian border. In his letter to the Secretary-General of 27 July 1992, Akashi warned that the Khmer Rouge "will feel the impact [of resolution 766] only when a stronger resolution is adopted by the Council" (United Nations 1995c, 206-208). Akashi argued the Khmer Rouge would be forced to adopt a more cooperative stance only when economic sanctions were combined with strengthened border checkpoints in areas adjacent to Khmer Rouge controlled areas. This would allow monitors to better "control the inflow of arms and petroleum and the outflow of gems and logs, a major source of [the Khmer Rouge's] income." (United Nations 1995c, 206-208)

Sanctions, however, would only be effective only with the cooperation of external actors, particularly regional actors. Akashi noted that Thailand could play a "key role" but doubted "the capacity of the Thai civilian government in Bangkok to impose its will upon Thai military in the border areas." (United Nations 1995c, 206-208) While Akashi acknowledged that China continued to hold the "confidence" of the Khmer Rouge, its "influence is probably diminishing since the cessation of its military assistance." (United Nations 1995c, 206-208) Other states also held potential sway over the Khmer Rouge: Indonesia (as co-Chair of PICC), Japan (for its "economic clout"), the US (for its "military and political weight"), and France (for its "historic ties"). However, it was not always clear that these states would support aid conditionality as a policy instrument. The Asian countries, particularly the members of ASEAN, seemed less inclined to support economic sanctions.

While the SOC, FUNCINPEC and the KPNLF cantoned forces and began the disarmament and demobilization process, the Khmer Rouge took advantage of the resulting power vacuum. As violence inside Cambodia increased, debate continued as to how best to address the situation. Some called for Security Council authorization of peace enforcement.[16] Most, however, including the P5, the Secretary-General, Sanderson, Akashi, and many troop-contributing countries, opposed authorization of the use of force (Brown and Zasloff 1998, 105; Heininger 1994, 67). There was little consensus on the role aid conditionality might play as part of a larger diplomatic strategy. While the US and UK called for economic sanctions, the Secretary-General opposed sanctions and encouraged "patient diplomacy" (S/24800, para. 25). Most ASEAN states opposed sanctions and some sought to accommodate the Khmer Rouge's complaints (Doyle and Suntharanlingam 1994; Doyle 1994).

While efforts to bring the Khmer Rouge back into the peace process continued, UNTAC worked to support implementation of the accords where it could. Resettlement of refugees and internally displaced persons continued. UNTAC also worked with the SNC to finalize Cambodia's election law. The final election law was adopted by the SNC, in the absence of the Khmer Rouge, on 5 August 1992. As provided for in the Paris Accords, representation in the Constituent Assembly would take place on a provincial basis. Each province was to be allocated electoral seats on the basis of population. Electors would be selected from party lists on the basis of the proportion of votes cast for each party in each province (Brown 1998). The SNC adopted a restrictive definition of the Cambodian voters, effectively disenfranchising ethnic Vietnamese residing in Cambodia. Potential voters were limited to persons born in Cambodia who had at least one parent born in Cambodia, or persons born outside Cambodia who had at least one parent born in Cambodia if that parent was also the child of at least one parent born in Cambodia. Polling stations were authorized in Europe, North America and Australia, but potential voters were required to return to Cambodia for registration (S/24578).

Provisional registration of political parties began on 15 August 1992. Those who sought to exercise this right, particularly supporters of parties seeking to organize in areas they did not control, were often the victims of political violence and intimidation. Because the SOC controlled 80 percent of Cambodia, FUNCINPEC and the KPNLF supporters were the most frequent victims. Party organizers were "harassed and reported to have been killed while attempting to open offices." (Lizée 2000, 111) UNTAC negotiated an agreement between the SOC, FUNCINPEC and the KPNLF which allowed competing parties to operate in one another's territory. This agreement went into effect on 10 September and helped to reduce some of the most overt forms of intimidation though those seeking to exercise political freedoms remained the target of violence and intimidation. The Secretary-General's second progress report on UNTAC of 21 September noted with concern that the Cambodian parties had taken few proactive measure to ensure implementation of Cambodia's human rights obligations, including civil and political rights (S/24578, para 28). Despite these concerns, preparations for elections continued.

The issue of Khmer Rouge non-compliance continued to dominate most discussions of Cambodia. The Thai and Japanese governments renewed their diplomatic imitative in August (S/24800, Annex I). As the Khmer Rouge continued to make demands outside the parameters of the Paris Agreements, the Australians put forward their own proposal, "Cambodia: next steps" on 16 September (United Nations 1995c). It called for a two-pronged approach to the situation in Cambodia. First, it outlined a series of steps designed to pressure the Khmer Rouge into fulfilling its obligations. First, the PICC co-chairs and representatives of the Khmer Rogue were to meet as provided for in article 29 of the Paris Agreement. The PICC co-chairs were to report the results of their consultations to the Security Council by mid-October. This would allow the outcome of the consultation to be known before the General Assembly was scheduled to authorize the second tranche of UNTAC funding. By the third week of October, the Security Council was asked to authorize sanctions against they the Khmer Rouge should it fail to comply with the Paris Agreements. If the Khmer Rouge had not met its obligations by 1 December 1992, it would not be allowed to participate in elections. ,

While acknowledging that the best possible alternative was full and complete implementation of the Paris Accords, the Australian proposal urged as complete implementation as possible in the event the Khmer Rouge was not persuaded to cooperate fully. To this end, elections were to go forward in those areas of Cambodia in which UNTAC operated. UNTAC's military component was to be redeployed to provide security should the Khmer Rouge act on its threats to disrupt the elections with violence. The Australian proposal also requested that funding to areas controlled by the SOC, FUNCINPEC and KPNLF be increased to prevent economic collapse and called for the creation of a dedicated radio station to improved UNTAC's communication with the Cambodian people.[17]

Portions of the Australian proposal were implemented on 13 October with the adoption of Security Council Resolution 783. In addition to demanding the Khmer Rouge "fulfill immediately its obligations under the Paris Agreements" (S/RES/783, para. 6), the Security Council approved plans to hold elections as planned and called on the Governments of Thailand and Japan and the PICC co-chairs to consult with the Khmer Rouge and report to the Secretary-General by 31 October. The Secretary-General was to report on the implementation process no later than 15 November at which time the Security Council would consider further measures. The Security Council further urged "all States, in particular neighboring countries, to provide assistance to UNTAC to ensure the effective implementation of the Paris Agreements." Resolution 783 also authorized the establishment of radio UNTAC, and urged speedy disbursement of aid pledged during the Tokyo Conference (S/RES/783). Under resolution 766, aid was not to benefit the Khmer Rouge.

Subsequent meetings between representatives of Thailand, Japan and the Khmer Rouge failed to make a breakthrough. Dumas and Alatas continued the diplomatic initiative in Beijing on 8 November 1992. Meeting with representatives of the SNC and Akashi, the PICC co-chairs outlined progress in the implementation process including voter and political party registration, refugee repatriation, and disbursement of funds for reconstruction and rehabilitation. The PICC co-chairs also summarized measures taken by UNTAC to address the concerns of the Cambodian parties. They encouraged all parties comply with the terms of the Paris Accords and stressed "that no party had the right to default on its obligations on the ground of complaints relating to the implementation of the plan. Such an attitude would not be tolerated." (S/24800, Annex III) The Khmer

Rouge responded by announcing that not only would it not participate in the demobilization process, it would not participate in elections.

By mid-November, the demobilization process was effectively suspended with only 25 percent of forces cantoned (S/24800). Cease-fire violations, primarily in the form of armed clashes between the Khmer Rouge and the SOC continued as did politically motivated attacks, primarily against FUNCINPEC and KPNLF supporters. Attacks against ethnic Vietnamese were also on the rise. In addition, UNTAC became a more frequent target of armed attacks. Small arms fire downed an UNTAC helicopter on 5 November. An electoral team and civilian police monitors came under attack two days later. UNTAC investigators attributed responsibility to the Khmer Rouge in both incidents. Despite the deteriorating situation on the ground, the Secretary-General continued to urge the Security Council to pursue "patient diplomacy" rather than adopt "specific measures to get [the Khmer Rouge] to honour its commitments." (S/24800, para. 24) Citing the cost of postponing elections and concerns that continued uncertainty would trigger outright collapse of the Cambodian economy; Boutros-Ghali continued to support plans to hold elections no later than May. Though the Paris Accords made no provision for the office, he also supported holding presidential elections at the same time. The PICC co-Chairs and the Secretary-General shared the opinion that such an election would "contribute to the process of national reconciliation and help to reinforce the climate of stability which will be needed during the delicate period when the Constituent Assembly will have the task of drafting and adopting the new Cambodian constitution." (S/24800, para. 21)[18]

On 30 November 1992, the Security Council adopted resolution 792. It called for elections for Cambodia's Constituent Assembly to go forward as planned in areas that UNTAC had "full and free access as of 31 January 1993." (S/RES/792) The Secretary-General was asked to submit a proposal for presidential elections for further consideration. In addition to condemning the Khmer Rouge's continued failure to meet its obligations under the Paris Accords, resolution 792 called for international support of the SNC's 22 September moratorium on the export of logs from Cambodia and asked for international cooperation to ensure petroleum did not reach territory controlled by the Khmer Rouge. The threat of a Chinese veto and need to avoid alienation of the Thai government, however, mitigated against mandatory sanctions (Findlay 1995, 43). Instead of the strong sanctions envisioned in the Australian proposal and encouraged in Akashi's letter to the Secretary-General, the Khmer Rouge was left with the warning that continued non-compliance would trigger further Security Council discussion, perhaps leading to a freeze of the Khmer Rouge's foreign held assets (S/RES/792).

The Thai government issued a formal response to resolution 792 the same day. It urged continued negotiations with the Khmer Rouge and noted that under the terms of the Paris Accords, border monitors were to be deployed "along the *Cambodian side of the border*." (S/24873) The Thai statement concluded,

As a member in good standing of the United Nations, Thailand will comply with measures that may have effect on Thailand so long as these measures do not contravene Thai law or Thai sovereignty and territorial integrity.

(S/24873)

Resolution 792, without mandatory sanctions and with less than enthusiastic support by the Thai government, did little to induce change in the Khmer Rouge's position.[19]

As the end of the year approached, the situation in Cambodia did not improve. On 1 December Khmer Rouge forces detained six UN military observers and shot at a helicopter that attempted to come to their aid. The following day six members of UNTAC were injured by a land mine (S/24884). The Khmer Rouge later released a statement which blamed UNTAC for the detention of the military observers. The statement argued that the incident was the result of the observers' attempt to enter Khmer Rouge-controlled territory without prior approval from the Khmer Rogue. Further, the Khmer Rouge accused UNTAC of engaging in "a smear campaign ... designed to mislead the United Nations Security Council into enforcing sanctions" against the Khmer Rouge (United Nations 1995c, 247). The Khmer Rouge repeated its offer to enter phase II of the demobilization process and honor the cease-fire on the condition that UNTAC verify the withdrawal and nonreturn of Vietnamese forces, and "control" the SOC administrative structure in cooperation with the SNC. The President of the Security Council responded with a condemnation of the Khmer Rouge's "illegal detention of UNTAC personnel" and demanded an end to such acts (S/25003).

UNTAC was not the only target of Khmer Rouge violence. Ethnic Vietnamese in Cambodia had long been victimized by the Khmer Rouge.[20] Anti-Vietnamese violence began in June and escalated at the end of 1992. Ethnic Vietnamese were killed in Tuk Meas village and in Koh Kong province in November. UNTAC investigations identified the Khmer Rouge as responsible for both attacks (S/24800). Four additional incidents took place in October and November. The Khmer Rouge was also blamed for a December attack of a Tonle Sap fishing village in which 14 were killed and 14 wounded (S/25154). The Vietnamese government demanded the SNC and members of the international community "take resolute measures so as to put an immediate end to these bloody acts."[21] UNTAC resisted pressure to provide direct protection and instead reminded the Cambodian parties of their obligation under the terms of the accords "to ensure law and order are maintained in the zone under its control ... and that human rights and fundamental freedoms are protected."[22] Few concrete measures were taken and racial violence continued.

As the security situation unraveled, UNTAC's Human Rights Component, supported by UNTAC's civilian police and other mission elements, worked to improve human rights conditions in Cambodia through education, observation, investigation, and advocacy. Though the SNC made formal commitments to meet international human rights standards in April 1992 and formally adopted resolutions consistent with these standards, they were never fully implemented.

UNTAC sponsored a number of initiatives in an effort to remedy the situation. It reviewed Cambodia's legal, judicial and penal systems, recommending changes in law, procedure and training. It secured the release of hundreds of prisoners, many of whom had been detained by SOC authorities without trial. UNTAC also helped secure the release of a KPNLF member of the SNC who had been arrested by SOC authorities under suspicious circumstances. As of September 1992, the Human Rights Division received 250 complaints including harassment, intimidation, arbitrary arrest, wrongful death, destruction of property and wrongful injury. Investigation found only 13 complaints to be unsubstantiated (S/24578). UNTAC frequently reminded the Cambodian parties of their obligation to ensure law and order, and to protect human rights and fundamental freedoms in territories under their control.

Despite its best efforts, Denis McNamara, Director of UNTAC's Human Rights Component, later reported that UNTAC received only "limited cooperation from most of the Cambodian leadership [...], and in many instances outright resistance, particularly in the human rights field." (1995, 59) While the Paris Accords authorized UNTAC to investigate complaints of human rights abuse and to take appropriate corrective action, "the exact dimensions of such activity were not detailed. Cambodian parties used this ambiguity to regularly contest UNTAC's investigations and proposed remedies for complaints." (Brown and Zasloff 1998, 118) Frustrated with the limited cooperation of the SOC and other local authorities and faced with increasingly violent human rights violations, UNTAC took the unprecedented step of assuming powers to arrest, detain and prosecute individuals suspected of human rights violations in early 1993 (S/25154).

The Secretary-General's Third Progress Report on UNTAC released 25 January 1993 identified three categories of violence of special concern. First on the list were politically motivated attacks. This included more than 40 attacks, some involving hand grenades and automatic weapons, in which supporters of FUNCINPEC and the Buddhist Liberal Democratic Party (the political party of the KPNLF) were the primary victims. Second on the list were attacks against ethnic Vietnamese. Third on the list were random killings intended to spread "a climate of fear and intimidation." The report criticized local administrative structures that had "not responded properly to their obligation to ensure respect for human rights and fundamental freedoms and to accept UNTAC control and supervision" (S/25154, para. 95). The report also notified the Security Council that phase II of the demobilization process had been officially suspended as a result of the dramatic increase in cease-fire violations and announced that UNTAC would give priority to protection of "freedom from intimidation, freedom of party affiliation and freedom of action of political parties" in an effort to ensure elections took place in a neutral political environment (S/25154, para. 101).

Violence initially declined in January but increased again in February. The Secretary-General's next report expressed particular concern for politically motivated violence in areas under SOC control. It noted, serious difficulties relating to the maintenance of law and order in the areas under its [SOC's] control and the protection of the staff and offices of other political parties engaged in lawful political activity.   (S/25289, para. 48)

Preparations for elections continued despite the violence and limited access to the estimated five percent of Cambodians who lived in Khmer Rouge-controlled territory. By the time voter registration ended in January 1993, 4.7 million voters (including 362,000 repatriated refugees and internally displaced persons) and 20 political parties had been registered (S/25719). The success of UNTAC's voter registration program, however, cannot be interpreted as acceptance of democratic norms and in some cases was the result of the SOC's effort to undermine the democratic process. Many SOC employees were required to join the CPP (the political party of the SOC) and register to vote. At the village level, SOC officials made villagers join the CPP and helped them to register to vote. They were then told that they must vote for the party to which they belonged. In response to this and other efforts to spread disinformation about the electoral process and intimidate voters, UNTAC launched an aggressive voter education campaign. Supplemented by Radio UNTAC and the distribution of radios by the Japanese government and NGOs in November 1992, the campaign emphasized the secrecy of the ballot (Ledgerwood 1996).

UNTAC faced a number of challenges as it sought to implement the Paris Peace Accords. In addition to problems of the different Cambodian factions spreading disinformation about UNTAC's mission and the electoral process, political violence remained a significant problem in early 1993. Because the SOC controlled 80 percent of Cambodian territory, UNTAC placed special emphasis on monitoring SOC authorities. Despite concerns raised by UNTAC and the Secretary-General, political violence and intimidation continued. "Between January and May 1993, the SOC's attacks caused more than 200 deaths" (Peou 2000, 173). The first two weeks of March alone were marked with 27 incidents of political violence. UNTAC investigators attributed 11 deaths to the SOC, 4 to the Khmer Rouge and one to FUNCINPEC. These figures do not include some 150 additional cases that remained unsolved (Ledgerwood 1996).

By March 1993 the primary goal of UNTAC became conducting elections and departing the country as scheduled. UNTAC's human rights component met with resistance from within UNTAC as some personnel argued it should take a "passive, less operational role" (McNamara 1995, 62) to facilitate cooperation by the parties to accomplish other aspects of the mandate. This attitude increased as the election date approached (Doyle 1995; Brown and Zasloff 1998).

On 8 March, the Security Council adopted Resolution 810 condemning the Khmer Rouge's continued failure to comply with the Paris Accords as well as attacks against UNTAC personnel, ethnic Vietnamese and Cambodia's other political parties. The Security Council called for elections to go ahead as scheduled and urged, all Cambodian parties to take all necessary measures to ensure freedom of speech, assembly and movement, as well as fair access to the media, including the press, television and radio, for all registered political parties during the electoral campaign starting on 7 April 1993, and to take all necessary steps to reassure the Cambodian people that the balloting for the election will be secret

(S/RES/810, para. 8)

The Cambodian parties were further reminded that UNTAC's mandate would expire three months following the creation of the Constituent Assembly. The goal of UNTAC's mission had clearly changed from building the liberal democracy promised in the Paris Peace Accords to holding elections which would mark the countdown to UNTAC's exit.

Two days after Resolution 810 was adopted by the Security Council, the Khmer Rouge attacked Chong Kneas, a fishing village on the Tonle Sap. 33 ethnic Vietnamese were killed and 26 injured (S/25409, Annex). This was the worst of a series of attacks that resulted in some 200 deaths and led 30,000 ethnic Vietnamese to leave the country. UNTAC naval forces escorted refugees to the Vietnamese border, but senior UNTAC officials were unwilling to take direct responsibility for the safety of ethnic Vietnamese inside Cambodia, emphasizing that it was the responsibility of local authorities to protect ethnic Vietnamese in areas under their control (S/25719). In a press conference two days following the massacre UNTAC's military commander told reporters. "We are here on peacekeeping, not [an] internal security mission" (Sanderson quoted in Jordens 1996, 147). Similarly, the UN naval commander in Siem Reap province expressed concern that the peacekeeping operation would turn into peace enforcement (Jordens 1996, 147).

The official campaign period began as scheduled on 7 April. Violence continued to be a problem and appeals by the European Community (S/25563, Annex) and other external supporters of Cambodia's peace process seemed to have little effect. The killing of a Japanese volunteer and his Cambodian translator on 8 April 1993 prompted 40 UN Volunteers to leave Cambodia (S/25719). Tensions increased on 13 April when the Khmer Rouge, citing security concerns but refusing UNTAC's offer to provide security, closed its Phnom Penh office and withdrew from the capital (United Nations 1995c, 282). The Khmer Rouge increased its efforts to disrupt elections. Between 27 March and 3 May 1993, eleven UNTAC civilian and military personnel were killed. Other members of UNTAC were taken hostage and later released (Heininger 1994). Despite these developments ASEAN[23] and the Security Council[24] urged elections take place as scheduled though the increased violence forced a reduction in the number of polling stations from 1900 to 1400 (Findlay 1995, 41; Akashi 1994). UNTAC also permitted the SOC, KPNLF and FUNCINPEC to engage the Khmer Rouge "in proportional response" in an effort to enhance security around polling stations (Findlay 1995; Akashi 1994).

As April came to a close, the signatory States of the Paris Agreements issued a statement on the implementation of the peace process in Cambodia and acts of violence. It supported the SNC's decision to go ahead with elections and called on UNTAC to "create and maintain a neutral political environment conducive to the holding of free and fair elections" (S/25658). The statement failed to hold the Cambodian parties, particularly the SOC, responsible for continuing political violence and intimidation, and ongoing human rights violations despite provisions of the Paris Accords that placed ultimate responsibility for law and order, and respect for human rights on local Cambodian authorities. The statement failed to meaningfully articulate the norms of embodied in the Paris Accords and failed to engage in strategic social construction through aid conditionality. Without strong international support for norm construction, Akashi adopted limited criteria for "free and fair elections". On 21 April 1993, Akashi announced that "freeness and fairness" of elections would be judged by,

> [t]he extent to which the campaign and voting are marred by violence, intimidation and harassment; the extent to which SOC, which controls the largest zones and has the most extensive administrative structure, enjoys unfair advantages, whether by using its administrative apparatus for its own political ends or by denying other political parties access to the public media; and the technical conduct of the poll. (S/25784)

The final assessment would be made after the election.

Despite ongoing political violence and the rise of banditry, official campaign meetings and rallies took place throughout Cambodia. There were "no reports of disruption or harassment and no clashes." (S/25719) However, the Secretary-General's Report of 3 May 1993 acknowledged that the SOC, FUNCINPEC and the KPNLF employed their respective administrative structures to promote political activities, and to monitor, harass, and intimidate political opponents (S/25719). In addition, there was some evidence that the parties were unwilling to hold their own supporters accountable for attacks against their political competitors. As with previous reports, the SOC was held responsible for a majority of incidents. The report concluded, "The Parties of FUNCINPEC and KPNLF must persist in their determination to campaign peacefully without giving in to intimidation." (S/25719/ para. 137).

As the campaign period continued intimidation and political violence continued. In addition, there were fundamental problems with ensuring that all political parties had freedom of movement and access to the media such that they were able to get their message to voters. Most media outlets were controlled by the SOC. FUNCINPEC's attempt to set up its own television transmitter ran into SOC opposition and delays. It was finally up and running only after UNTAC intervention on its behalf. The SOC also refused to allow Prince Ranariddh's personal plane use of Cambodian airports despite UNTAC's insistence that he be allowed to do so (Jeldres 1993). The smaller parties met even more difficulty in their attempt to get their message out. While Radio UNTAC broadcast programming to counter government hegemony over the media, this effort was far short of granting all political parties free and equal access to the media as a whole.

The campaign period officially ended on 19 May 1993, allowing a four-day cooling off period. Despite imperfections in the electoral campaign period, over 200 political rallies and meetings took place. "In nearly every case, parties complied with UN electoral law and security regulations. No reports of disruption or harassment and no clashes." (S/25719) Despite the Khmer Rouge's threats of violence and call to boycott the elections, 4.2 million Cambodians (89 percent of registered voters) participated in relatively peaceful elections between 23 and 27 May 1993.[25] Akashi declared the elections to have been "free and fair, despite some harassment, hindrances and pressure" on 29 May 1993 (Akashi 1994, 206). Overall, UNTAC found voters had participated "without fear in an atmosphere of calm that was almost completely free of violence and intimidation. There was no significant disruption of the polling." (S/25879, Annex) There were some technical difficulties. For example, some of the seals on ballot boxes were ruptured due to rough roads and in some cases pencils were used instead of ink. Most issues were resolved by monitors on the spot (S/25879, Annex).

Post-Election Cambodia

Despite the success of balloting process, post-election Cambodia was marked with continuing uncertainty. As Reginald Austin, head of the UN Electoral Component, commented, "The Paris Peace Agreements are completely vacuous on the post election environment." (cited in Roberts 2001, 118) Missing from discussions prior to elections were: 1) the role of a loyal opposition in the new government; 2) the capacity of FUNCINPEC to rule; and 3) the CPP's willingness to relinquish power. As a result, the peace agreement did not include, "contingencies for either the division or sharing of power." (Curtis 1998, 17) Without agreement on how power would be transferred or shared, the durability of the transition ushered in by the Paris Accords was highly uncertain.

The balloting process was scarcely completed before a new controversy erupted. The CPP began a campaign to discredit the election process charging fraud, poor administration, and bias. CPP party leaders demanded that UNTAC repeat elections in seven provinces but produced little evidence of electoral irregularities (Brown and Zasloff 1998). UNTAC investigated specific complaints on the spot and offered further investigation by a third party. Hun Sen declined to cooperate with this process and "ominously mentioned a possible bloody revolt by [the] CPP." (Akashi 1994, 207) Newspapers reported CPP predictions of "bloodshed and secessionism unless its demand for an inquiry into alleged poll fraud was granted." Further, the CPP "declared its refusal to 'hand over power until the UN investigate[d] the allegations of malpractice'." (Roberts 1998, 18)

While the CPP continued to argue that electoral irregularities invalidated the final tally, UNTAC's daily vote count predicted the FUNCINPEC would win by a plurality. In Akashi's view even if the CPP's allegations were true, they would not affect the outcome of elections. UNTAC continued to post daily vote counts despite CPP opposition (Boutros-Ghali 1995b, 46). On 31 May, "Phnom Penh was paralyzed by rumors that a special squad from the Ministry of National Security was about to arrest the FUNCINPEC leadership as well as the heads of the local human rights and student groups." (Jeldres 1993, 112) That same day, Prince Norodom Chakrapong, Deputy Prime Minister of the SOC, led a succession movement in seven eastern provinces. UNTAC personnel withdrew from these areas after their offices were attacked and they were threatened with violence.[26]

Before all the ballots were counted, the CPP's Chea Sim and Hun Sen asked Sihanouk "to assume absolute power so as to avoid post-election violence." (Curtis 1998, 10) On 3 June Sihanouk announced the formation of the "National Government of Cambodia" which was to include participation of the CPP, the KPNLF, FUNCINPEC and the Khmer Rouge. Sihanouk was to serve as head of state, prime minister and commander of the armed forces and police. FUNCINPEC's Prince Ranariddh and the CPP's Hun Sen were to serve as deputy premiers. France supported Sihanouk's initiative but the proposal was withdrawn once the US, China, Australia, Britain and FUNCINPEC's Ranariddh objected (Brown 1998; Curtis 1998; Roberts 1998).[27]

With most international supporters insisting that all parties accept the election results as endorsed by the Security Council as a condition of future aid, final election results were announced on 10 June 1993 (Boyce 2002, 28-29). FUNCINPEC won 58 seats in the Constituent Assembly, the CPP 51, the BLDP 10, and MOLINAKA 1 (Brown 1998). Under the terms of the Paris Accords, the new constitution had to be approved by a two-thirds majority of the Constituent Assembly. Cambodia's new constitution would, therefore, require the support of both FUNCINPEC and the CPP. The Constituent Assembly was sworn in on 14 June 1993. Its first act was to proclaim Sihanouk Head of State and conferred to him "full and special powers inherent in his capacity and duties as Head of State in order that he may save [the Cambodian] nation." (cited in Lizée 2000, 126) Son Sann of the Buddhist Liberal Democratic Party (BLDP/KPNLF) became the Assembly's first President.

The election results were formally endorsed by the Security Council on 15 June 1993 (S/RES 840) The leaders of the succession movement in the eastern provinces fled to Vietnam that same day. The following day, Sihanouk announced the formation of the Interim Joint Administration despite the fact there was no provision for an interim government in the Paris Accords. Ranariddh and Hun Sen were named Co-Chairmen of the Council of Ministers (Brown and Zasloff 1998). Although FUNCINPEC won a plurality of the vote, the events of the post-election period demonstrated the political reality that the CPP would seek "more real power in the new government than it had actually won (or been given by the Cambodian people)." (Curtis 1998, 11-12) Akashi accepted the formation of the Interim Joint Administration as the only practical alternative:

> One can question the legitimacy and stability of this formula, which treated the two major parties on an approximately equal basis. While this is unorthodox by universal democratic principles, we have to admit the practical wisdom of combining the 'new wind', represented by the victorious FUNCINPEC, consisting mostly of upper and upper middle class intellectuals aspiring to the restoration of the monarchy, with the experience, and power of CPP, which is authoritarian but has 14 years of administrative experience, with much of the army and the police under its control.   (Akashi 1994, 207)[28]

Representatives of the United Nations and key states "played down" this departure from the Paris Accords (Findlay 1995). ASEAN formally voiced its support of the interim government on 22 July 1993 (Boutros-Ghali 1995c; Curtis 1998). That same month the Security Council approved $20 million in emergency financial aid for Cambodia (Boutros-Ghali 1995c). The UN provided the Interim Joint Administration $10 million (most of which was donated by Japan) to support administrative, police and military integration (Findlay 1995, 92-93).

With the Constituent Assembly installed, a 13-member committee was assigned the task of drafting Cambodia's new constitution. Sihanouk made clear that he did not want foreigners involved in the drafting process and the committee met behind closed doors. As a result UNTAC had little real input (Curtis 1998; McNamara 1995). UNTAC took a "hands off approach," limiting itself to offering technical assistance, primarily in the form of organizing seminars on different constitutional structures and making constitutional scholars available for consultation (Findlay 1995). UNTAC's human rights component drafted a proposed Bill of Rights but did not insist upon its acceptance (Brown and Zasloff 1998, 194-194).

The Security Council confirmed UNTAC's limited role on 27 August 1993 when it adopted Resolution 860. Despite the incomplete implementation of the Paris Accords and the fact that "many of the key elements and institutions needed to support a liberal democracy governed by the rule of law were still obviously lacking," Resolution 860 confirmed UNTAC's mandate was to end with the creation of a government under Cambodia's new constitution (McNamara 1995, 79). The only exception was the Security Council's authorization of some mine clearance, military police and medical personnel to remain through the end of November to support the integration of forces and to provide technical training (S/RES/860; Boutros-Ghali 1995c).

In September, Norodom Ranariddh and Hun Sen traveled to Pyongyang where they met with Sihanouk. They carried with them two draft constitutions. One would establish a constitutional monarchy; the other, a republic. Sihanouk chose constitutional monarchy. This meeting was followed by the first public debates of the draft constitution in the Constitutional Assembly. After five days of debate, the new constitution was adopted. 113 voted in favor, 5 against, with two abstentions. Cambodia became a constitutional monarchy on 24 September 1993 (S/26529).

The new government adopted a complex system of power sharing. Though members of the BLDP and MOLINAKA were awarded some minor positions in the new government, most important positions were shared by the CPP and FUNCINPEC. Norodom Ranariddh became First Prime Minister. Hun Sen was named Second Prime Minister. Ranarridh and Hun Sen were also named Co-ministers of Defense and Interior (Internal Security) (Brown and Zasloff 1998). Despite FUNCINPEC's plurality in the elections, FUNCINPEC and the CPP headed 10 government ministries each. Co-ministers and vice-ministers from FUNCINPEC and the CPP were assigned to the Ministry of Defence and Interior. Other ministries were divided such that the appointment of a Minister from the CPP was always accompanied with the appointment of a Vice-Minister of the FUNCINPEC and *vice versa*. An under-secretary from each of the major parties was also named in each ministry (Curtis 1998; Brown and Zasloff 1998).

To a certain degree, power sharing was also extended to the provincial level. FUNCINPEC won the plurality of votes in four provinces, including three of the five most politically and economically important. The CPP won five provinces, including three of the four politically and economically least important. The CPP retained control of the post of governor in these provinces but allowed FUNCINPEC to name governors for the five provinces won by the CPP. The posts of first vice-governor and second vice-governor were split between the two parties. Because the elections were national and not local, FUNCINPEC held less than 20 percent of district and local positions (Roberts 2001). Real power remained with the CPP through its control of the state bureaucracy and provincial structures, including the police, the army, the judiciary, and tax collection (Curtis 1998; Doyle 2001, 90-91).

Within a week of the formal adoption of the constitution, Akashi and Sanderson declared UNTAC's mission complete and left the country (Kamm 1998). The process of withdrawing UNTAC personnel had begun in early August. Staff from UNTAC's Repatriation and Electoral Division departed upon completion of their mission elements. One of the few provisions of the Paris Accords that extended beyond adoption of the new constitution was for continued human rights monitoring. The appointment of a Special Rapporteur for this purpose met resistance from regional states. As a compromise a Special Representative for Human Rights, without an explicit monitoring role, was dispatched. The UN Human Rights Office in Cambodia opened on 1 October 1993 (McNamara 1995). The UN would have a continued presence through the involvement of its agencies in reconstruction and development efforts. Indonesian diplomat Benny Widyono was appointed to represent the Secretary-General in Cambodia and to coordinate the overall UN presence in April 1994 (Boutros-Ghali 1995b).

Cambodia Under The New Constitution

Although the elections for Cambodia's Constitutional Assembly were declared 'free and fair' by Akashi and the new constitution was approved by two-thirds of the Constitutional Assembly as required in the Paris Accords, Cambodia did not experience a transition to durable peace. The Khmer Rouge abandoned the peace process and returned to armed conflict before elections took place. For those parties that did participate in UN-sponsored elections, the end result was little more than an uneasy system of power sharing which would breakdown into open political violence in less than five years. Though the Khmer Rouge was the greatest external threat to the peace, "the greater threat to the stability of the fragile new quasi-democracy was the tensions between Hun Sen and Ranariddh." (Brown and Zasloff 1998) Formally, FUNCINPEC and KPNLF armed forces joined those of the SOC to create the Royal Armed Forces of Cambodia which was charged with the task of defending the new Cambodian political order from the Khmer Rouge.[29] Informally, each party sought to retain the loyalty of its armed forces and political funcitonaries. Political violence and intimidation continued to characterize the relationship between the participants in Cambodia's fragile coalition government. Between 1993 and 1997, Cambodia experienced four failed coups. The coup of June 1997 finally succeeded in removing Ranariddh from power (Doyle 2001).

Despite provisions in the new Constitution that seemed to embrace liberal democracy, Cambodia retained many characteristics of a one-party state including intolerance of "any kind of opposition or dissent" (Curtis 1998, 26). Neither Sihanouk nor Hun Sen showed much interest in implementing the new constitution. Both engaged in a grab for power and money "while stripping away the thin overlay of democracy imparted by the U.N. peacekeeping mission." (Gray 1996) Although the constitution provided for two three-month session per year, the National Assembly met infrequently (Brown 1998). Son Soubert, a member of the National Assembly at the time, recalled only two pieces of legislation in the first year: a national budget and a plan for the reorganization of the government's finances (Kamm 1994, 1998). When the National Assembly did meet, debate was generally absent (Roberts 2001).[30] The National Assembly served largely as a rubber-stamp for policies already approved by the FUNCINPEC-CPP leadership. In addition, the Constitutional Court was never established and the judiciary remained highly politicized. Anti-corruption laws were never sent to the legislature.

Without a strong opposition party, criticism of the new government found expression in press accounts of government corruption and other misdeeds. The government responded by confiscating printed material and closing down some publications. In the first two years following the withdrawal of UNTAC, "at least three journalists who had published accounts of official corruption were killed." (Brown and Zasloff 1998, 208) No arrests or charges were made. Sihanouk and Hun Sen worked together to pass a "draconian press law" in mid-1995

(Lizée 2000, 155). The new law prohibited the publication of "articles which jeopardize national security, and political stability." It also made the publication of articles "defaming politicians" a criminal offense (Ojendal 2001, 311, emphasis added).

The decline in human rights conditions, particularly respect of civil and political rights, was noted by both the US Department of State and Amnesty International. Concerns raised in the 1995 US State Department Report on Human Rights were echoed in Amnesty International's 1996 report,[31]

> 1995 saw a steady deterioration in the human rights situation in Cambodia; political violence returned to the capital Phnom Penh, prisoners of conscience were detained in the country's prisons and newspaper editors were put on trial for expressing their opinions, as the attitude of the Royal Government of Cambodia to political opponents became increasingly intolerant. Prominent government critics were threatened and intimidated.
>
> (cited in Brown and Zasloff 1998, 294)

The government generally ignored these reports. Soldiers and police were rarely prosecuted for their abuses (Gottesman 2003; Brown and Zasloff 1998).

Advocates of democratic reform were especially targeted for acts of political violence and intimidation. In her 1995 *New York Times* article, Barbara Crossette reported on life in "newly democratic Cambodia,"

> The offices of a struggling independent newspaper are ransacked by ax-wielding villagers, and the Prime Minister applauds. A new opposition party is declared illegal before it is formally launched. Grenades explode at the office of another independent-minded senior politician, and in the courtyard of a Buddhist temple that has been sheltering his supporters.
>
> (quoted in Brown and Zasloff 1998, 228-229)

Crossette's "independent-minded senior politician" was likely the BLDP's Son Sann. In 1995 two BLDP supporters were killed and thirty injured in a grenade attack on BLDP headquarters. Many more were injured when the military broke-up an "illegal" BLDP political rally (Brown and Zasloff 1998).

The BLDP was not the only critic of the Ranariddh-Hun Sen alliance. One of the most consistently outspoken critics of the anti-democratic tendencies of the new government was Sam Rainsy who served as one of FUNCINPEC's representative on the SNC and was the new government's original Minister of Finance. He was removed from office following his public objections to the decision by Ranariddh and Hun Sen to move control of logging from the finance ministry to the military. Long a critic of high level government corruption, he publicly urged donor states to make aid conditional on "greater transparency in public decision-making" (cited in Brown and Zasloff 1998, 226). Sam Rainsy was subsequently expelled from FUNCINPEC for "breach of party discipline" (Brown and Zasloff 1998, 241). Arguing that Sam Rainsy was awarded his position in the National Assembly by merit of his membership in FUNCINPEC,

Ranariddh also had him expelled from the National Assembly. While, UNTAC's electoral rules required all *candidates* be a member of a legally registered political party, the rules for expulsion from the National Assembly were vague. When the issue came before the National Assembly, Chea Sim, who regularly chaired its meetings was absent; An aide reported that he was "'embarrassed' by the whole affair." (quoted in Brown and Zasloff 1998, 241-242) The acting chair refused to recognize members who wished to discuss the matter. The motion to expel Sam Rainsy was quickly passed by an overwhelming majority on 22 June 1995 (Brown and Zasloff 1998).[32]

Ranariddh justified his actions in a 3 August 1995 statement:

> Sam Rainsy had been given ample warnings, friendly lectures and gentle persuasions to mend his wayward ways and toe the FUNCINPEC party line. We must not forget the Royal Government is a coalition government. As such, FUNCINPEC Party members must resolve any issues within the party apparatus and not fight in public, giving unwarranted advantages to undesirable elements. In any political organization, party loyalty and allegiance to the leadership, especially the President, is a pre-requisite to party unity and stability. Disloyalty, resorting to blatant lies and demagogy to further enhance one's career is not within the interest of the party or the nation. As for expulsion from the National Assembly, it is FUNCINPEC's right under UNTAC law and the internal regulations of the National Assembly which is a sovereign and independent organization.   (quoted in Brown and Zasloff 1998, 243)

Once out of office, Sam Rainsy sought to create a formal opposition party, the Khmer National Party (KNP). The KNP was denied legal status by the government and party organizers and supporters were subject to threats, intimidation and violence.[33] In an effort to gain legal acceptance, the KNP formed an alliance with one of the many Cambodian parties that had gained legal standing prior to the 1993 elections but did not win a seat in the newly formed National Assembly. The Cambodian government, through an Interior Ministry directive, responded by ordering all political parties, except the four represented in the National Assembly at the time, to close their offices and cease operations. Additionally, the government required provincial authorities to report activities of local and international non-governmental organizations (Agence France Presse 1996).

Both Ranariddh and Hun Sen defended the actions of the Cambodian government during this period with the argument that "democracy *per se* ... was not the most pressing need now for Cambodia, and that foreigners should not have opinions on this" (Ojendal, 2001, 208). Echoing the "Asian Values" argument of political leaders in of Malaysia and Singapore, they justified their actions by arguing that political stability and economic development ought to be given priority at the expense of free speech, free association and political debate (Asiaweek 1994).

Cambodia's financial benefactors were divided over aid policy. For some donors, the need to support the FUNCINPEC-CPP government as a bulwark against the Khmer Rouge outweighed any interest in the development of democratic norms of political legitimacy. France and the United States officials publicly expressed concern that Cambodian officials were giving insufficient attention to the development of democratic and human rights norms in Cambodian society. At the same time they signaled that aid policy might be reconsidered.[34] The mere suggestion of aid conditionality was vehemently criticized by Hun Sen as an inappropriate intrusion in Cambodia's internal affairs (British Broadcasting Corporation 1995b; 1995c; 1996). In his view, conditioning foreign aid on democratic development or human rights inside Cambodia constituted foreign interference in Cambodia's domestic affairs. Hun Sen gave a series of public speeches (some broadcast on Cambodian Radio) in which he defiantly noted,

> I am fed up with the world expressing alarming fear over Cambodia's internal affairs. It is really terrible. Let me say this to the world: Whether you want to give aid to Cambodia is up to you, but do not discuss Cambodian affairs too much. (quoted in Ojendal 2001, 313)

In contrast, Japan and the ASEAN states formed the largest group of donors and investors in Cambodia and shared their belief that it was inappropriate to condition their aid and investment decisions on democratic or human rights criteria (Peou 2000).[35] Hun Sen praised Japan and other Asian states who refused to tie aid to human rights or political conditions inside Cambodia. For example, in a 4 December 1995 address on Radio Phnom Penh, Hun Sen concluded his speech with praise for Japan's aid policy,

> We should not oppose Japan because it has never intervened. Japan is very good. Aid from Japan is completely unconditional. Apart from Japan, it is really an awful mess. (quoted in Brown and Zasloff 1998, 248)

The international community remained divided in its response to political developments inside Cambodia. Despite its poor democratic and human rights record, including passage of the 1995 press law, the ouster of Sam Rainsy and increasing levels of violence directed against would-be political opponents, total aid disbursements to Cambodia actually increased from 1995 to 1996. Bilateral aid in 1996 increased by 13 percent over 1995 levels with Japan and France, Cambodia's two largest aid donors contributing $111 million and $43 million, respectively (Peou 2000, 376).[36] The only donor to decrease aid in 1996 was the IMF which did not release balance-of-payments support due more to the Cambodian government's reluctance to adopt transparent economic policy than democratic or human rights conditions (Peou 2000, 376).

The 1997 Coup

The rise in political violence between those who participated in UNTAC-sponsored elections can be understood only in reference to the collapse of the Khmer Rouge. The trickle of Khmer Rouge defections that began during the transition period increased to a stream in 1994. In February alone, 3,000 Khmer Rouge soldiers defected. This number increased dramatically in July 1994 when the Khmer Rouge was officially outlawed and its members offered amnesty. As experienced soldiers left the Khmer Rouge, they were actively recruited by both the CPP and FUNCINPEC. By 1996 relations between the CPP and FUNCINPEC had deteriorated significantly. Forces loyal to the two factions engaged in armed clashes and rumors of an attempted coup circulated in the Spring of 1996 (Doyle 2001).

In early 1997 Ranariddh joined with Sam Rainsy's KNP to form the National United Front (NUF). The NUF called for a single prime minister, anti-corruption measures, and recovery of state property that had found its way into the hands of CPP supporters (Peou 2000). The KNP was said to have 250,000 members and its coalition with FUNCINPEC was a significant threat to the CPP as the country began to look forward to the 1998 elections. The KNP became the target of a renewed campaign of political violence and intimidation. Under the direction of the CPP, grenades were thrown into the crowd during a political rally on 30 March 1997. Sixteen were killed and nearly two hundred wounded (Brown and Zasloff 1998, 259). In May 1997, the KNP sponsored a peaceful demonstration calling for the creation of an independent judiciary as provided for in the 1993 constitution. At least fifteen died and over one hundred were injured when two men threw grenades at demonstrators; Journalists seem to have been particularly targeted in the attack (Doyle 2001). Witnesses report that CPP armed forces allowed the assailants to escape (Kamm 1998).

In May CPP bodyguards announced they had uncovered a plot to assassinate Hun Sen (Doyle 2001, 91). Throughout the Spring of 1997 "bodyguards" loyal to FUNCINPEC and the CPP fought in the streets of Phnom Penh. The clashes involved 800-1,000 men armed with APCs, tanks, and rockets (Kamm 1998; Peou 1998). Similar battles occurred in June (Doyle 2001, 91). Sensing impending crisis, Cambodia's major donors met in early July.[37] Discussions emphasized the need for political stability as a prerequisite to long-term economic development as well as the donor's desire that the Cambodian government increase the amount of internally generated revenue and improve transparency in the government budget (Lizée 1997). While the meeting's final statement emphasized the need for Cambodia to continue on the democratic path, "a close reading of what the international community basically wanted did not contribute to further democratization." (Peou 2000, 379) In line with the "Asian Values" argument expressed by its leading members, the Consultative Group identified "Political stability for economic development [as] their top concern." (Peou 2000, 379) Political stability, not full implementation of the constitution, was the condition for further financial support (Peou 2000, 380). Donors also encouraged the government "tighten its budget." (Peou 2000, 380)

Shortly thereafter, Hun Sen took definitive action against FUNCINPEC. Following rumors of an alliance between Ranariddh and the former Khmer Rouge leader Khieu Samphan, Ranariddh was formally removed from office the weekend of 5-6 July 1996. (Doyle 2001; Brown and Zasloff 1998). The UN Center for Human Rights in Cambodia reported that close to 100 military and FUNCINPEC officials loyal to Ranariddh were summarily executed, some after being tortured (Peou 1998). Hundreds more were arrested (Ott 1997). It is believed the weekend of fighting resulted in 150 deaths (Curtis 1998, 49). Opposition television and radio were seized (Brown 1998). Most of the senior leadership of FUNCINPEC and the Khmer Nation Party were killed or fled the country (Doyle 2001). Ranariddh avoided this fate as he had left the country two days prior "to see relatives" in France. The coup was followed by a purge of diplomats, civil servants, and political appointees loyal to FUNCINPEC (Brown and Zasloff 1998, 262). By the end of the year, 50,000 Cambodians sought refuge on the Thai border. General Niek Bun Chhay led a military resistance of FUNCINPEC and Khmer Rouge fighters (Doyle 2001, 93). On 9 July a government white paper was released. It justified the removal of Ranariddh from office due to his "policy of provocation." It charged that Ranariddh redeployed security forces to the capital without Ministry of Defense approval, increased their number with Khmer Rouge elements, illegally imported weapons for these forces, and that Ranariddh had created a coalition "in clear opposition to the CPP" (Curtis 1998, 51). Ranariddh and other FUNCINPEC officials were also charged with openly criticizing the coalition government and the CPP." (Peou, 2000) These charges were likely true.[38]

In violation of party by-laws and the Cambodian constitution, FUNCINPEC's Ung Huot was selected to replace Ranariddh as First Prime Minister on 6 August. The National Assembly vote was 86 for, 4 against, with 6 abstentions, and 3 spoiled ballots. Only 99 of the Assembly's 120 members participated; the rest fled the country or were in hiding (Brown and Zasloff 1998, 264). Assembly members reported feeling pressure to vote in favor of Ung Huot as demanded by Hun Sen and were not confident of the secrecy of the ballot (Peou, 2000). Those who opposed were threatened. Say Bory, Secretary of State for Relations with Parliament, is quoted, "'Opposing Hun Sen's politics puts your life at risk,' said Say Bory, ... I asked him whether he meant his political life. 'No.' he replied firmly." (Kamm 1998, 232)[39] Following the coup against Ranariddh, "Constitutional procedures and effective government ground to a halt; neither the cabinet nor the National Assembly met." (Doyle 2001, 91)

The July 1997 coup and related violations of democratic and human rights norms was triggered by a number of factors, not least of all was the underdevelopment of democratic norms of political legitimacy. The creation of the NUF threatened the CPP's political chances at the polls. Public opinion polls conducted in early 1997 indicated the CPP had only 20 percent support in the countryside, its base of support in the 1993 UN-sponsored elections (Doyle

2001). The stakes of the 1998 election were even higher than those of 1993 because the Cambodian constitution stipulated that a single prime minister would be selected in the 1998 election (Brown and Zasloff 1998). Writing for the *Phnom Penh Post* in 1996, Jamie Factor described the CPP as "uncomfortable with elections and with voluntary persuasion, and they regard the use of force as an acceptable political strategy." (quoted in Brown and Zasloff 1998, 224) The CPP under Hun Sen's leadership was simply unwilling to risk defeat at the polls and retained the will and the means to hold onto power by force.

The July donors meeting may have served to encourage Hun Sen's move against his political rival. The donors' demand that public spending be reduced has significant implications in Cambodia's politically charged environment. Patron-client relationship were a fact of political life in Cambodia. Civil service employment and political appointments had long been often used to reward political loyalty. Following the 1993 elections, the public payroll was simply expanded to create positions for the supporters of FUNCINPEC and other opposition parties. The demand to reduce state expenditures translated to firing political supporters. Given its limited popular support, the CPP could ill-afford to alienate the party faithful with economic layoffs. The CPP needed to be firmly in charge so that it could meet the demands of external donors by laying off non-CPP civil servants. It is probably not just coincidence that Hun Sen justified his actions as an effort to maintain political stability (Peou 2000).

The International Response

With nearly two-thirds of its annual revenue from foreign aid, the Cambodian government should have been extremely vulnerable to the credible threat of economic sanctions. But, as with the response of the international community to previous violations of democratic and human rights norms, the international community did not use aid conditionality to insist the Cambodian constitution be fully implemented in response to the events of 1997. In the immediate aftermath of the coup, the United States reduced aid by two-thirds, cutting off all but humanitarian assistance (Ott 1997, 436). The World Bank, the IMF, Australia, and the EU also initially froze non-humanitarian aid (Doyle 2001). France and China sharing the view that Hun Sen was "the only guarantor of stability in Cambodia" were reluctant to endorse a settlement that required the return of Ranariddh (Lizée 2000). In fact, no country "called publicly for the reinstatement of Prince Norodom Ranariddh." (Richardson 1997a) The United Nations Security Council encouraged Ranariddh and Hun Sen to find a political settlement but did not condemn either side (Peou 2000). On 26 November 1997, the UN General Assembly called for "free, fair, and credible elections" by March 1998 (Haq 1997). Japan, Cambodia's largest donor, initially suspended aid but reinstated it before the month's end after officially accepting Hun Sen's argument that Ranariddh "pursued a strategy of provocation" and thus Hun Sen was "justified in his actions." (Schear 1996, 396)[40] The Japanese government pledged to maintain existing aid programs noting "Hun Sen had promised to preserve the democratic institutions and coalition government set up in 1993." (Lizée 2000)

Generally speaking, Asian countries including China, Japan, and the members of ASEAN expressed concern that aid conditionality would "set a dangerous precedent of foreign interference in internal affairs" (Richardson 1997b). In their view such action would make Hun Sen "intransigent, isolating Cambodia and adding to instability in the region." (Richardson 1997a) Malaysian Foreign Minister and Chair of ASEAN's standing committee, Abdullah Ahmad Bandai, acknowledged the violence was "unfortunate" but "would not insist on his [Prince Ranariddh's] return to power if Hun Sen maintained, as he had done, the coalition arrangement which had been set up in 1993." (Lizée 2000, 158)[41] Following US pressure, ASEAN postponed plans to extend membership to Cambodia (Brown and Zasloff 1998). The ASEAN states appointed the foreign ministers of Indonesia, Thailand, and the Philippines to mediate talks between ASEAN and Hun Sen to ensure elections were held in 1998 (Lizée 2000). This effort was backed by donor demands that "some resemblance of democracy [be] restored." (Abdullah quoted in McPhedran) The World Bank and the Asian Development Bank put new aid on holding pending a political solution.

> [M]ajor Japanese-financed infrastructure projects were stalled in the pipeline, ostensibly due to the deteriorated security situation: 'We said, "We can't send out engineers",' a Japanese official explained, 'but we're very sure that he [Hun Sen] understood the real reasons.' (Boyce 2002, 31)

Australia and Canada agreed to restore aid only if Ranariddh and other opposition leaders were allowed to compete in the 1998 elections (Peou 1998). In the end, agreement was reached only after Japan helped to broker a settlement. Ranariddh was to be convicted of his crimes and immediately granted a royal pardon. Only then would he be permitted to participate in the 1998 elections (Peou 2000). Prince Ranriddh and other opposition leaders would return to Cambodia under international guarantees of safety (Neou and Gallup 1999, 153).

As Cambodia prepared for the 1998 elections, CPP party loyalists were accused of manipulating the electoral commission (Peou 2000). Political supporters of competing parties were subject to violence, intimidation and in some instances torture (Sanderson and Maley 1998). Five million Cambodians participated in the balloting process with no reports of violence or intimidation. The elections were monitored by 500 observers from the UN-coordinated Joint International Observer Group which declared the elections "free and fair" (Seper 1998). Human Rights Watch and other groups that looked beyond the day of polling, however, challenged this conclusion. In their view, pre-election violence and intimidation undermined the credibility of their finding (Shawcross 1998; Seper 1998).

The CPP won 64 seats in the National Assembly with 41 percent of the popular vote. FUNCINPEC won 43 seats, and the Sam Rainsy Party 15 (Brown, 1993; Peou 2000). The Cambodian constitution required "important questions" to be passed by a two-thirds majority. The CPP's plurality was insufficient to control the National Assembly and the CPP offered to create a new CPP-FUNCINPEC coalition government. FUNCINPEC, charging polling irregularities, initially refused to accept the election results and turned down the CPP's coalition offer. Eight hundred complaints of irregularities were submitted to the National Election Committee (NEC). The NEC, however, dominated by CPP supporters, refused to transparently address allegations of polling irregularities (Peou 1998). This led to public protests that came to an end following "violent crackdowns from government police" (Peou 2000, 319). In November, Hun Sen emerged as the sole Prime Minister heading a new FUNCINPEC-CPP coalition government. Ranariddh would serve as chairman of the National Assembly (Doyle 2001, 93). The Sam Rainsy Party was left out of power entirely (Peou 2000, 319).

Political development in Cambodia since the 1998 election has been uneven. On one hand, as President of the Center for Social Development, Chea Vunnath noted "independent thinkers still live on the edge of danger here, where politically inspired assassinations are a fact of life – and death." (cited in Crossette 2003) Cambodia's legal system remains politicized and "geographically inaccessible and prohibitively expensive" for most Cambodians. Further, members of the military and police "are never prosecuted for abuses, prompting nongovernmental organizations to write lengthy reports on the problem of impunity — reports that are themselves ignored." (Gottesman 2003, 355) On the other hand, Cambodia has a lively newspaper trade and urban Cambodians "are not afraid to voice their strong political views." (Crossette 2003) Cambodia's first-ever elections at the district and local level were held in 2002 bringing greater political pluralism to local governance. Cambodian NGOs such as the Center for Social Development conduct independent research on Cambodian social issues and held "town hall" meetings to encourage ordinary Cambodians to participate in the political process as the country prepared for another round of national elections in July 2003. The 2003 National Assembly elections were again marked by allegations of impropriety and disputes over elections results delayed the formation of the new ruling alliance for nearly three months. In the end, the CPP was awarded 73 seats, FUNCINPEC 26, and the Sam Rainsy Party 24 (Sambath 2003).

Peacebuilding Without Constructing Democratic Norms

UN peacebuilding is premised on the idea that liberal democracy – a political system in which social actors compete for political influence in representative institutions through the exercise of free speech, free press, and nonviolent political organization under the rule of law – is better suited than other forms of governance to manage social conflict without recourse to violence. The Cambodian peace process failed, however, to produce the political transformation envisioned in the Paris Accords. Large-scale armed conflict involving the Khmer Rouge ended not as a result of the peace process but as a result of its internal collapse. Political violence remained a characteristic of relations between the parties that participated in UN-sponsored elections; Episodic large-scale violence ended only after the CPP consolidated power in the aftermath of the 1997 coup. Although the peace process led to several positive changes in Cambodia including the return of refugees and internally displaced persons and the creation of limited space for independent political organization and human rights activism, political violence and intimidation remain the final arbitrar of political relations. Despite the amazing logistical success of the UNTAC-organized elections, they proved insufficient to institutionalize liberal democracy in such a way that it could effectively manage civil conflict and delegitimize political violence and intimidation.

While there were many factors that led to this outcome, one of the most striking features of the Cambodian peace process was the failure of external supporters of the Paris Accords to insist upon the full implementation of the Accords during the transition period or the full implementation of the constitution once it was adopted by the Constitutional Assembly. Granted, short of military intervention, there may have been little that could have been done to secure the cooperation of the Khmer Rouge and this had significant consequences for demobilization. However, more might have been done to ensure the protection of human rights and the creation of a neutral political environment in areas under the control of the CPP, FUNCINPEC and the KPNLF. In Finnemore and Sikkink's model, the construction of new political norms begin when norm entrepreneurs articulate new norms of political legitimacy. In the Cambodian case, two normative systems were articulated. The Paris Accords embodied a set of liberal democratic norms which emphasized the illegitimacy of political violence and intimidation, and envisioned a transition to a system of representative government in which individual civil and political rights were to be protected under the rule of law. UNTAC was mandated to facilitate the transition to a political system informed by liberal democratic norms.

However, UNTAC's efforts to engage in norm articulation and strategic social construction were limited by the normative values of some of the operation's largest donors and the international community's general reluctance to engage in strategic social construction. As implementation of the peace accords met with resistance from inside Cambodia, Japan and the member states of ASEAN proved more inclined to support political stability and the principle of non-intervention than to support the construction of liberal democracy through insisting the Cambodians protect human rights, including civil and political rights, in areas under their control. As influence shifted from UNTAC to regional actors, the potential that Cambodian would evolve into "soft authoritarianism" or "guided democracy" increased (Ojendal 2001, 304). In fact, ASEAN

states were inclined to defend Cambodia from criticism of its democratization
and human rights record.

> A distinguished Southeast Asian diplomat serving in Cambodia advanced the
> premise that Western embassies were unrealistic in pressing Cambodia to reach
> a multiparty democracy. (The Cambodian constitution, he asserted, is 'pie in
> the sky.') This Western brand of democracy was not suitable for Cambodia, he
> argued. Westerners were too prone to criticize Cambodia (and other Southeast
> Asian nations) for abridging freedom of the press and abusing human rights...
> Forwarding an argument similar to that of Singapore's Lee Kuan Yew and Ma-
> laysia's Dr. Mahathis Mohamad, the diplomat continued to argue that donors
> should be more concerned with economic development rather than individual
> rights.   (Brown 1998, 294)[42]

The Cambodian adoption of an Asian model of democracy can be traced to as
early as 1994 when (shortly after dismissing Sam Rainsy as well as Commerce
Minister Va Huot and Agriculture Minister Sam O) Ranariddh told reporters,
"Rather than having France as a model, it's better to have a development model
such as Singapore." (Asiaweek 1994)

Anecdotal evidence suggests that the Cambodian leadership might have
more fully honored the accords and more fully implemented the Cambodian
constitution if faced with consistent demands to do so from the donor community. Boyce, the leading expert on "peace-conditionality" argues that aid conditionality played an important but limited role in the Cambodian peace process.

> During the UNTAC period, aid helped to maintain the balance of power be-
> tween the CPP and Funcinpec, despite the KR's abandonment of the peace
> agreements. After the 1993 elections, the Core Group of donor governments
> used conditionality to bring the CPP into a coalition government. When the
> coalition collapsed and violence broke out in 1997, aid conditionality again
> helped to pave the way for new elections and a return to coalition rule in 1998.
>   (Boyce 2002, 31-32)

Others, have argued that international monitoring, another factor is strategic
social construction, was a factor in improving human rights conditions in Cambodia. Gottesman, for example, notes that at the time of the UNTAC operation,
"Cambodians were protected against human rights abuses in direct proportion to
the pressure placed upon the SOC by the international community and the ability
of UNTAC to monitor events in Cambodia." (2003, 348) By the same token,
lack of strong criticism backed by material consequences may have contributed
to the abuse of power. Son Soubert, for example, blamed "the lack of a strong
international opposition to Hun Sen's bullying" for his later abuses of power,
including the 1997 coup (quoted in Crossette 2003). This evidence suggests that
something more closely approximating a liberal democracy in Cambodia might
have been created if aid donors were more willing to engage in strategic social
construction. However, key external supporters of the Cambodian peace process
did not fully endorse liberal democracy as a requirement of internal peace in

Cambodian and proved unwilling to condition aid on this requirement. So long influential external supporters of the peace process, particularly Cambodia's largest financial donors did not insist upon complete implementation of the Paris Accords, including its human rights provisions, Cambodian leaders were able resist external efforts to construct new political norms. One can only speculate how events in Cambodia might have unfolded if international actors had adopted policies more in accord with the Finnemore and Sikkink model of norm construction.

Notes

1. The case study draws from the work of Brown (1998), Curtis (1998), Doyle (1995; 1995), Kiernan (1993b), Peou (2000), Prasad (2001), Ratner (1993a) and The United Nations (1995c). UN documents are available in The United Nations (1995c).

2. Sihanouk held the title "king" from 1941 to 1955 and again from 1993 to 2004. In 1955 he abdicated in favor of his father Norodom Suramarit but served as Prime Minister and Foreign Minister. He became Cambodia's Head of State following his father's death in 1960 but retained the title "prince" until 1993.

3. Also see UN documents A/RES/41/6, A/RES/40/7, A/RES/39/5, A/RES/38/3. A/RES/37/6, A/RES/36/5, and A/RES/35/6.

4. See Prasad (2001) for complete copy of the text.

5. Text of the P5 Framework Document of 28 August 1990 is reprinted in UN document A/45/472-S/21689.

6. Text of the Joint Statement of the Informal Meeting on Cambodia is reprinted in UN document S/45/490-S/21732, Annex. The Framework Document was subsequently endorsed by the General Assembly on 15 October 1990 (A/45/3).

7. Reprinted in UN document A/46/61-S/22059, Annex II.

8. Also see Evans (1994) and Ratner (1993a).

9. Texts of the Paris Peace Agreements are included in UN document A/46/608-S/23177. The 19 state signatories were: Australia, Brunei Darussalam, Cambodia (i.e. the SNC led by Sihanouk), Canada, the People's Republic of China, the French Republic, the Republic of India, the Republic of Indonesia, Japan, the Lao People's Democratic Republic, Malaysia, the Republic of the Philippines, the Republic of Singapore, the Kingdom of Thailand, the Union of Soviet Socialist Republics, the United Kingdom of Great Britain and Northern Ireland, the United States of America, the Socialist Republic of Vietnam and Yugoslavia (as the Chairman of the Non-Aligned Movement).

10. Cambodians who exercised their new right to free speech to protest government corruption were soon targeted by SOC authorities. One victim of the contradiction was Cambodian-American Vanna Om Strinko who returned to Cambodia with the intention of establishing an independent political party, the New Life Democratic Party. She became the target of intimidation by SOC authorities and was prevented by police and SOC undercover agents from making a public announcement about her party. When UN officials raised her case with Sihanouk in November 1991, he urged all factions adhere to the peace accords though little changed in the actual behavior of the Cambodian leaders or their followers (Agence France Presse 1991g).

11. Additional international instruments addressing the rights of women, children and refugees; and the prohibition of torture were signed in September 1992 (Heininger 1994).

12. UNTAC had no official contingency plans if one of the parties did not uphold the accords. Boutros-Ghali argued that such measures would have demonstrated "bad faith" and "could have undermined the UN's role in implementing the agreements." (Boutros-Ghali quoted in Heininger 1994, 43)

13. See UN document A/47/285-S/24183, Annex I.

14. See UN document A/47/285-S/24183, Annex II.

15. This emphasis on sovereignty and unwillingness to link aid to activity internal to Cambodia is consistent with values articulated in the Bangkok Declaration issued at the Regional Meeting for Asia of the World Conference on Human Rights (Spring 1993). The Declaration, "[d]iscourage[d] any attempt to use human rights as a conditionality for extending development assistance [and emphasized] the principles of respect for national sovereignty and territorial integrity as well as non-interference in the internal affairs of States, and the non-use of human rights as an instrument of political pressure." (A/CONF.157/ASRM/8) State participants included: Bahrain, Bangladesh, Bhutan, Brunei Darussalam, China, Cyprus, Democratic People's Republic of Korea, Fiji, India, Indonesia, Iran, Iraq, Japan, Kiribati, Kuwait, Laos, Malaysia, Maldives, Mongolia, Myanmar, Nepal, Oman, Pakistan, Papua New Guinea, Philippines, Republic of Korea, Samoa, Singapore, Solomon Islands, Sri Lanka, Syria, Thailand, United Arab Emirates, and Viet Nam (A/CONF.157/ASRM/8). For discussion of ASEAN's use of the principle of non-interference see Ramcharan (2000).

16. General Loridon, Deputy Military Commander of UNTAC, was dismissed after he advocated the use of force against the Khmer Rouge (Findlay 1995, 37).

17. The need for UNTAC to have a direct, uncensored means of communicating with the Cambodian people was deemed vital to the success of the operation. Not only did UNTAC have to contend with the Khmer Rouge spreading disinformation about its mission, it also needed to counter misinformation from the SOC and others about the election process. For example, voter registration levels were particularly high in SOC controlled areas in part because many state employees were required to join the CPP and register to vote. In some cases, SOC village officials made villagers members of the CPP and helped them register to vote. These new party members were told that they must vote for the party to which they belonged. UNTAC voter education, supplemented by Radio UNTAC and the distribution of radios by the Japanese government and NGOs in November 1992, emphasized the secrecy of the ballot to counter the government's campaign of misinformation (Ledgerwood 1996).

18. Though the Paris Accords made no provision for an office of president the issue was discussed through 1992 and was supported at different time by the Sihanouk, FUNCINPEC, the SOC, and the KPNLF, and ASEAN. Boutros-Ghali endorsed the proposal that presidential elections be held at the same time as elections for the Constitutional Assembly following endorsement by Sihanouk and approved by FUNCINPEC, the KPNLF, and the SOC (S/24800). In February 1993, Sihanouk announced that presidential elections should take place after Cambodia's new constitution had been adopted (S/25273). Sihanouk was the only candidate every publicly mentioned for this office.

19. The Thai government did join Laos and Vietnam in a ban on log imports from Cambodia effective 1 January 1993. However, UNTAC reported "numerous and large-

scale violations" as the SOC, Khmer Rouge and FUNCINPEC continued log exports despite the official ban (S/25289).

20. Other Cambodian factions also engaged in anti-Vietnamese rhetoric. Early in the UNTAC operation, Hun Sen notified UNTAC personnel that "UNTAC police would have to intervene, not my police" should ethnic Vietnamese be victimized by the opposition (quoted in Jordens 1996, 143).

21. See Letter dated 30 December 1992 from Mr. Nguyen Manh Cam, Minister of Foreign Affairs of Viet Nam, to the Secretary-General concerning violence against Vietnamese residents in Cambodia (S/250503).

22. See Letter dated 28 January 1993 from the Secretary-General to Prince Norodom Ranariddh, member of the Supreme National Council, concerning the situation in Cambodia and the role of UNTAC and Letter dated 29 January 1993 from the Secretary-General to Mr. Hun Sen, member of the Supreme National Council, referring to letter of 5 January 1993 concerning the situation in Cambodia (United Nations 1995c, 268).

23. Letter dated 18 May 1993 from Singapore transmitting statement by the ASEAN Foreign Ministers on the elections in Cambodia (S/25794).

24. S/RES/826 (1993), 20 May 1993.

25. On 28 January 1993, the SNC announced that elections would take place between 23 and 25 May 1993. The election period was later extended to 27 May to ensure all registered voters had an opportunity to cast their ballot (S/25289).

26. Whether or not the CPP leadership in Phnom Penh directed the succession or it was the result of a local initiative by party faithful is debated. What is known is that Sanderson and other members of UNTAC believed Hun Sen was responsible and intended to use it to wrest power from FUNCINPEC (Curtis 1998).

27. US diplomats threatened to withdraw US aid if the Khmer Rouge was included in the new government (Doyle and Suzuki 1995). American opposition could be reversed if the Khmer Rouge "complied with certain conditions, including disarming, granting free access to their zones, and ceasing military operations against the other factions" (Jeldres 1993, 114).

28. In a later interview the Barbara Crossette, Akashi indicated that the compromise was "Cambodia's choice. He drew what he saw as a parallel with the U.S. occupation of Japan after World War II and later Japanese alternation to the system Americans created to illustrate that outsiders don't always have solutions totally acceptable to local people." (2003)

29. Continuing conflict with the Khmer Rouge displaced 79,842 Cambodian civilians in 1993 and as many as 50,000 refugees sought shelter along the Thai border in April 1994 (Peou 2000, 239; Doyle 2001).

30. Also see Gray (1996), Gottesman (2003) and Jeldres (1996).

31. Amnesty International, "Kingdom of Cambodia: Diminishing Respect for Human Rights," (May 1996).

32. Prince Sirividh (Sihanouk's half-brother) resigned his position in sympathy with Sam Rainsy. Sirividh was later placed under house arrest and later exiled following accusations that he was part of a plot to assassinate Hun Sen (Sanderson and Maley 1998).

33. The KNP was the only party to receive support of the US-based International Republican Institute (IRI). The IRI stopped working with FUNCINPEC, and the CPP in early 1996 after determining the groups were no longer democratic. The IRI's democratic

counterpart, the National Democratic Institute for International Affairs suspended operations in Cambodia in 1995 for similar reasons (Brown and Zasloff 1998, 243-244).

34. However, these states did not coherently link these concerns to aid and other forms of economic assistance to Cambodia. For example, shortly after Sam Rainsy was expelled from the National Assembly in June 1995, the US House voted to grant Cambodia Most-Favored-Nation status.

35. Japanese policy continues in this direction. Speaking to reporters prior to the 1999 donors' conference, the Japanese Premier's deputy press secretary Akitaka Saiki noted, "Stability in Cambodia is Tokyo's priority ... as far as the Japanese government is concerned, we are of the position that we will not speak out on a domestic matter of another independent state." (Williams 1999) Also see Kakuchi (1999) and Johnson (1999).

36. Ott cites Japanese grants and technical assistance to Cambodia in 1996 at $152 million (1997, 436).

37. The Consultative Group Meeting (formally the ICORC) met on 1-2 July 1997. The ICORC became the Consultative group in 1996 marking the transition from a focus on short-term aid to long-term development assistance.

38. See Kamm (1998) and Brown (1998).

39. Also see Gottesman (2003).

40. Also see Neou and Gallup (1999, 153) and Ott (1997).

41. Also see British Broadcasting Corporation (1997) and Agence France Presse (1997).

42. Also see Hood (1998).

Chapter 4

Constructing Peace

Civil conflict remains one of the most significant threats to peace and security in the contemporary era. Historically, violent civil conflict has been more likely to end with the military victory of one side and the defeat of the other. Civil wars that end in this manner are "often associated with widespread human rights abuses, atrocities, genocide, environmental degradation and a host of other ills." (King 1997, 12) These nasty side-effects pose the potential for serious problems for those directly affected by conflict as well as regional and global actors affected by their negative transnational effects. Regional and international actors have a vested interest in developing techniques that aid the implementation of negotiated settlements to civil conflict that lead to the durable transformation of violent political conflict. As democratic and human rights norms have been adopted as the international standard of political legitimacy,[1] such efforts regularly include measures to promote human rights and democracy as part of a comprehensive conflict transformation strategy.

Since 1989, United Nations peacebuilding operations have been fielded in a number of countries to assist the implementation of negotiated settlements to civil conflict. UN peacebuilding operations are distinctive because they combine military and civilian mission elements. The military component is tasked with monitoring cease-fires and facilitating the disarmament, demobilization and reintegration process. The civilian component performs a number of tasks including refugee resettlement assistance, post-conflict rehabilitation, as well as promotion of democracy and human rights. These operations, however, have had substantially different results. Operations in El Salvador and Mozambique did contribute to durable conflict transformation. While admittedly, poverty and violent crime remain significant problems in both countries, violent political conflict has come to an end. Many of the reforms implemented during the operation continue to shape the development of political life. Other peacebuilding operations have produced less durable transformations. In Angola, there was a return to armed conflict even before the ballot count was completed. In Cambodia, despite UNTAC's significant contribution to the resettlement of refugees and internally displaced persons, the Khmer Rouge withdrew from the peace process prior to elections. Those parties that did participate in UN-sponsored elections continued to use violence and intimidation as a political instrument during and after the implementation period. One of the key differences between cases is the degree to which the implementation process was supported by a strategy of norm construction consistent with that described by Finnemore and Sikkink. Those cases that seem to have had the most successful, durable transformation of conflict included peace agreements that were interpreted to provide a consistent normative framework. That framework in turn was supported by strategic social construction. Where peacebuilding failed to produce durable transformations, the normative framework was undermined by competing interpretations and/or aid policy was not insist upon compliance with the formal terms of the accords.

El Salvador

In the Salvadoran case, norm articulators began to spin a web of norms that was logically consistent with an assisted transition to pluralist democracy long before fruitful negotiations between the Salvadoran parties began. As early as 1983, the Contadora Group worked to convince the governments of Central America to engage in processes of democratization and national reconciliation. This initiative was supported by formal statements and resolutions of the UN General Assembly, the UN Security Council and the Organization of American States. All reinforced the conceptual relationship between peace, democracy, human rights, and development. With the creation of the Support Group in 1985 and the formal acceptance of Esquipulas II by the Central American Presidents in 1987, both the idea that civil conflict was a legitimate matter of international concern and that such a conflict could and should be resolved by means of national reconciliation were firmly established.

By 1989 both the Salvadoran government and the FMLN were publicly committed to end the conflict and participate with their former enemy in democratic political processes. This, however, was not enough to generate a successful indigenous peace process. Distrust and insecurity remained significant stumbling blocks. The United Nations Secretariat — supported rhetorically and materially by formal and informal groupings of international and regional actors including the Contadora Group, the Support Group, the Friends of the Secretary-General, the OAS, the UN General Assembly and the UN Security Council — played an instrumental role in overcoming these impediments. Following the finalization of the Geneva and Caracas Agreements in 1990 and with the support of key states, UN officials came to be accepted as authoritative mediators of the Salvadoran peace process. External actors reinforced the authority and negotiating leverage of UN officials vis-à-vis the Salvadoran parties. The 1992 Chapultepec Accords were the outcome of a mediation process in which key international actors ensured the conflict transformation strategy included promotion of internationally accepted human rights and democratic norms.

With the formal terms of peace signed, peacebuilders were deployed to facilitate and monitor the implementation phase of the peace process. ONUSAL contributed to the durable transformation of conflict in El Salvador by utilizing peacebuilding strategies consistent with Finnemore and Sikkink's model of norm construction. Strategic social construction occurred repeatedly in the Salvadoran case. When one of the Salvadoran parties engaged in non-compliant behavior ONUSAL and other supporters of the peace process clearly communicated that specific actions violated the terms of the peace accords and specified necessary changes. Norm articulation was followed by offers of enabling aid and/or coercive aid conditionality. In most cases, this strategy succeeded in keeping the implementation process on track. Challenges to the peace process including disputes over demobilization, the terms of the land reform program, and delayed and incomplete implementation of the *Ad Hoc* Commission and Truth Commission reports were overcome by strategic social construction. Over time, the Salvadoran parties came to understand that access to international aid was shaped by ONUSAL's reports; flagrant violations of the accords had financial and political consequences. Donors responded positively to ONUSAL's requests of technical assistance and other forms of enabling aid. Positive reports by UN monitors translated to foreign aid in the form of grants and loans, which were the primary source of financing for many of the programs mandated by the peace accords (Boyce 1995). Donors also proved willing to withhold aid to punish non-compliance. Negative reports from ONUSAL brought international pressure and limited access to bi-lateral aid.[2]

As the peace accords were implemented, the Salvadoran parties' calculation of interest also changed as predicted by the Finnemore and Sikkink model. This was demonstrated most concretely when one of the FMLN's constituent groups, the FPL, admitted that efforts to maintain its capacity for armed conflict undermined its appeal as a political party. Though the initial discovery of the arms cache was accidental, it led to extensive cooperation between the FMLN and ONUSAL and the surrender of additional arms. Implementation of the accords also changed the balance of power between the Salvadoran parties. The international community's insistence that key provisions of the accords be implemented helped to sustain the peace process.

Unlike most peacebuilding operations to date, the 1994 elections did not mark the end of UN participation in the Salvadoran peace process. Under the terms of the peace accords, ONUSAL was mandated to verify implementation of *all* aspects of the accords. Following elections, outstanding issues included reforms of the judiciary, the civilian police, and the land tenure system. Reform continued within the Salvadoran legal and political system as former guerillas became members of the National Assembly. ONUSAL's reports continued to serve as a litmus test of progress and as an unofficial gatekeeper for foreign aid. After the elections, the newly installed ARENA-led coalition government was bolstered by its cooperation with the international community. Reports of human rights abuses and renewed political violence led to joint-investigations by the post-election government and external experts. Official impunity came to an end as police and military officials were charged for their participation in organized crime and other acts of violence. The norms constructed as part of the Salvadoran peace process had become self-sustaining; El Salvador had reached the third and final phase of the Finnemore and Sikkink model.

Despite delayed and incomplete implementation of the peace accords, ONUSAL and subsequent UN operations did facilitate the durable transformation of El Salvador's civil war through the social construction of new norms of political legitimacy. As the provisions of the Chapultepec Accords were implemented, the statements and actions of political actors began to indicate that the web of norms associated with liberal democracy – pluralism, free speech, political debate, compromise, and delegitimization of political violence – were taking hold. Over time, patterns of behavior that supported and helped sustain El Salvador's new norms of political legitimacy emerged beyond what could be accounted for by short-term interests manipulated by conditions imposed by foreign donors. The durability of the Salvadoran transformation following the withdrawal of United Nations peacebuilders is the most powerful indication that the norms articulated and strategically constructed during the peacebuilding operations have indeed become self-sustaining. UN peacebuilding in El Salvador has resulted in durable conflict transformation. Years after the departure of UN peacebuilders, many provisions of the accords remain in place. Most importantly, there has not been a large-scale return to political violence.

Cambodia

Whereas third-party support of the peace process in El Salvador incorporated norm articulation and strategic social construction, peacebuilding in Cambodia followed a very different path. Efforts to find a negotiated settlement between Cambodia's armed factions began at the behest of their external supporters at the end of the Cold War. Representatives of the Coalition Government of Democratic Kampuchea and the People's Republic of Kampuchea attended their first official meeting in late 1987. In 1988 indirect talks between the four Cambodian factions took place at the Joint Informal Meeting (JIM I). These talks produced agreement in principle to the withdrawal of foreign forces after which national elections would establish a new Cambodian government. There was no agreement, however, on specific measures to establish pacific relations between the

Cambodian factions or the nature of their post-conflict relationship. Sihanouk's dissatisfaction with the ASEAN-mediated process led to the involvement of other international actors. While the French and Indonesian foreign ministers officially served as co-chairs of the Paris International Conference on Cambodia (PICC), key negotiations also took place separately between the P5 and the Cambodian parties. The Secretary-General's Special Representative for Cambodia, rather than serving as the final mediator and later interpreter of the peace accords as was the case in El Salvador, competed for influence with the P5, ASEAN, and other interested states. In addition to the Agreement on a Comprehensive Settlement of the Cambodia Conflict, the accords also included the Agreement Concerning the Sovereignty, Independence and Territorial Integrity and Inviolability, Neutrality and National Unity of Cambodia. This second agreement undermined the implementation of the first due to emphasis on the obligation of all signators to "refrain from interference in any form whatsoever, whether direct or indirect, in the internal affairs of Cambodia" (Art. 2, Para. 2(b)).[3] This provision was not surprising given the illiberal character of several key participants in the negotiation process, particularly China and many of the ASEAN states. Without a shared normative framework and agreement to engage in strategic social construction, third-party supporters of the Cambodian peace process sometimes worked at cross-purposes. Key donors proved willing to ignore violations of democratic and human rights norms. In the end, the Paris Accords did not bring an end to the use of violence and intimidation as normal instruments of political power in Cambodia.

Negotiated settlements to civil conflict are notoriously difficult to implement. As the balance of power between the domestic parties to the conflict shifts as a result of the implementation process itself, it is increasingly important that third-parties "cultivate ripeness" to keep the peace process on track (Hampson 1996). The process of norm construction described by Finnemore and Sikkink is one means by which third-party supporters of peace process can cultivate ripeness and support durable conflict transformation. Challenges to the Salvadoran peace process were managed within the normative framework of the Chapultepec Accords; ONUSAL served as the authoritative interpreter of the accords and was aided in this role by key regional and international actors who supported its efforts with strategic social construction. In contrast, challenges to the Cambodian peace process were managed outside the normative framework of the Paris Accords in large part because Cambodia's largest donors proved unwilling to insist upon comprehensive implementation of the accords. The ASEAN states and Japan were committed to the principle of non-intervention and proved unwilling to make democracy or human rights a condition for aid. The first major crisis in the Cambodian peace process arose amidst cease-fire violations. The Khmer Rouge, in violation of the accords, refused to allow UNTAC personnel access to territory under its control. Whereas in the Salvadoran case, similar incidents were met with reassertion of the provisions of the negotiated settlement, recommendations as to what modifications were required to re-establish compliance, enabling and/or coercive uses of aid to facilitate compliance, and re-negotiation of the implementation timetable, the situation in Cambodia evolved into a standoff between UNTAC and the Khmer Rouge. Japan and Thailand sought to mediate a settlement but the situation continued to deteriorate. In the end the Khmer Rouge withdrew from the peace process entirely. This first major breakdown of the peace process was soon followed by the Tokyo Ministerial Conference on Rehabilitation and Reconstruction of Cambodia. The Tokyo Declaration made no reference to sanctions or the possibility that future aid would be available only to those in compliance with the Paris Accords.

Despite the Khmer Rouge's defection, the peace process continued. UNTAC's efforts to promote human rights and ensure all Cambodians could freely and securely participate in the political process were often met by resistance from the Cambodian factions, particularly the CPP. Key donor states came to view stability in the face of a resurgent Khmer Rouge as an acceptable trade-off for complete implementation of the democratic and human rights provisions of the accords. So long as the CPP stood as a credible force to contain the Khmer Rouge and prevent its return to power, many states unwilling to give any more than lip service to UNTAC's complaints. The few times that aid was used to leverage compliance with the terms of the Paris Accords, it did seem to be effective. Most strikingly, the CPP's initial refusal to accept UNTAC-sanctioned election results was overcome when key donors made it clear that those who contested the official results would be denied aid (Boyce 2002, 28-29). The results were soon accepted and a CPP-FUNCINPEC coalition was quickly formed.

UNTAC's ability to influence the implementation of the accords diminished significantly in the post-election period. Although Cambodia's new constitution did include many of the human rights and democratic provisions described in the Paris Accords, they were never fully implemented by the CPP-FUNCINPEC government. Cambodia's new leaders remained intolerant of opposition or dissent. Both Ranariddh and Hun Sen defended their actions with the same "Asian Values" arguments of Malaysian and Singaporean political leaders. Political stability and economic development were prioritized at the expense of liberal democratic values of free speech, free association and political debate (Asiaweek 1994). Both asserted a vision of Cambodian sovereignty which viewed attempts to link foreign aid to democracy or human rights as illegitimate foreign interference in Cambodia's domestic affairs (Ojendal 2001, 313). Japan and other Asian states, including Cambodia's largest aid donors and investors were praised for their respect of Cambodian sovereignty (Brown and Zasloff 1998, 248). Aid continued to flow despite the internal collapse of the Khmer Rouge in 1996, ongoing human rights violations, and overt political violence and intimidation. While aid was briefly suspended following the 1997 coup, it soon resumed with no significant consequences for the CPP. Violence and intimidation remain a normal part of Cambodian political life.

Conclusion

The studies of UN peacebuilding operations in Cambodia and El Salvador contained in the preceding chapters suggest that when third-party supporters of peace processes engage in norm articulation and aid conditionality consistent with the Finnemore and Sikkink model of norm construction, durable conflict transformation can be achieved. In the first phase of norm construction, norm entrepreneurs articulate new norms of political legitimacy. In the case of UN peacebuilding operations new norms are enshrined in the formal terms of peace. Where peace operations have contributed to the durable transformation of violent conflict, UN peacebuilders and other norm entrepreneurs have advocated a strategy of conflict transformation guided by democratic and human rights norms including: pluralism, the right to political participation, the right to free speech, the right to free press, the rule of law, and delegitimation of political violence. In the second phase of norm construction, norm articulation is combined with strategic social construction. Third-parties use aid conditionality to promote adherence to new norms. Aid is used as a carrot to reward cooperation and encourage compliance. Financial and technical aid supports capacity building which in turn enables implementation of the formal terms of peace. In addition, aid is used as a stick to punish parties that violate the formal terms of peace and the newly constructed norms they embody. In the final phase of norm construction, newly constructed norms become self-sustaining as socially constructed identities, interests and social networks are adapted to the logic of the new normative framework. It is only at this point that third-parties can end the process of strategic social construction with the expectation that their efforts might result in the durable transformation of violent conflict.

Comparison of the Salvadoran and Cambodian peace processes reveals that United Nations peacebuilding operations facilitated durable conflict transformation when implementation was supported with aid conditionality. In the Salvadoran case, UN peacebuilders and other third-party supporters of the peace process adopted mediation and implementation strategies consistent with the Finnemore and Sikkink model. The reports of ONUSAL and the UN Secretary-General were accepted as the authoritative interpretation of the Chapultepec accords. Donors supported construction of the normative framework embedded in the accords by deferring to ONUSAL's interpretation of the accords and imposing aid conditionality to secure the cooperation of the Salvadoran parties. UN peacebuilding in El Salvador contributed to the durable transformation of that conflict. In contrast, the Cambodian peace process diverged from the model described by Finnemore and Sikkink on two counts. First, third-parties did not insist upon the norms articulated in the Paris Peace Agreements. When the implementation of the peace accord as interpreted by UNTAC was resisted by the various Cambodian parties, noncompliance was "managed outside the guidelines ... of the UN-sponsored peace accords." (Munck and Kumar 1995, 165) Second, the largest financial contributors to the peace process were unwilling to employ aid conditionality as part of a larger implementation strategy. The Asian states were particularly reluctant to make aid contingent on compliance with the democratic and human rights provisions of the peace accords. In the end, UN peacebuilding failed to achieve the intended goal of ending political violence in Cambodia. To the extent civil conflict did come to an end, it was the result of the internal disintegration of the Khmer Rouge and the ability of forces loyal to Hun Sen to dominate Cambodia's institutional life, including the state bureaucracy, judiciary, police and military. Cambodia's civil war ended with the victory of one side over its enemies with the accompanying human rights abuses and "other ills" predicted by King (1997).

The cases of UN peacebuilding in El Salvador and Cambodia highlight the limited capacity of United Nations peacebuilders to transform civil war. To the extent peacebuilders have any capacity at all it is "on loan" from donor states. In El Salvador, where ONUSAL's interpretation of the peace accords were supplemented by strategic social construction, there was more complete implementation of the accords. Durable conflict transformation was a direct result of this process. In Cambodia, UNTAC was unable to secure sufficient compliance with the terms of the accords to bring about a sustained transformation. Peace agreements are never self-implementing and even negotiated settlements can face significant challenges. These challenges, however, need not derail the peace process. If peacebuilders are supported by external actors able and willing to engage in the process of norm construction, including articulation of a single post-conflict normative framework and willingness to engage in strategic social construction, they can help to realize durable conflict transformation.

Notes

1. Donnelly argues that international legitimacy has come to be linked with economic growth ("development'), popular political participation ("democracy"), and respect for rights of citizens ("human rights"). (Donnelly 2003, 185) Elsewhere Donnelly defines liberal democracy as "a very specific kind of government in which the morally and politically prior rights of citizens (and the requirement of the rule of law) limit the range of democratic decision making. Democracy and human rights are, therefore, mutually reinforcing in contemporary liberal democracies" (Donnelly 2003, 192).
2. While bi-lateral aid was withheld by donors engaging in strategic social construction, most international economic institutions did not employ a strategy of peace conditionality; loan conditionality sometimes worked at cross-purposes with peace conditionality and at times undermined the implementation of the Chapultepec Accords. Also see Boyce (1995; 2002).
3. This position is consistent with the Bangkok Declaration (1993) in which Asian states "Discourage[d] any attempt to use human rights as a conditionality for extending development assistance" and "Emphasize[d] the principles of respect for national sovereignty

and territorial integrity as well as noninterference in the internal affairs of States, and the non use of human rights as an instrument of political pressure." (A/CONF.157/ASRM/8)

Bibliography

Adibe, Clement E. 1998. Accepting External Authority in Peace-Maintenance. In *The Politics of Peace-Maintenance*, edited by J. Chopra. Boulder: Lynne Rienner.

Agence France Presse. 1991a. Cambodian Meeting Ends on Deadlock Over Electoral System. *Agence France Presse*, August 29, 1991. Available from Lexis-Nexis, http://www.lexisnexis.com. Accessed July 8, 2003.

———. 1991b. Cambodian Peace Accord Likely to be Signed October 31. *Agence France Presse*, September 21, 1991. Available from Lexis-Nexis, http://www.lexisnexis.com. Accessed July 8, 2003.

———. 1991c. Sihanouk Announced Agreement on Demobilisation, Powersharing. *Agence France Presse*, August 27, 1991. Available from Lexis-Nexis, http://www.lexisnexis.com. Accessed July 8, 2003.

———. 1991d. Sihanouk Urges Cambodian Factions to Adhere to Peace Accord. *Agence France Presse*, November 9, 1991. Available from Lexis-Nexis, http://www.lexisnexis.com. Accessed July 8, 2003.

———. 1992a. France Calls for Meeting in Tokyo to Examine Sanctions Against Khmer Rouge. *Agence France Presse*, June 18, 1992. Available from Lexis-Nexis, http://www.lexisnexis.com. Accessed July 8, 2003.

———. 1992b. New Cambodia Talks Aim to Resolve Khmer Rouge Impasse. *Agence France Presse*, June 22, 1992. Available from Lexis-Nexis, http://www.lexisnexis.com. Accessed July 8, 2003.

———. 1992c. Pessimistic SNC meets as Khmer Rouge Makes New Demands. *Agence France Presse*, June 10, 1992. Available from Lexis-Nexis, http://www.lexisnexis.com. Accessed July 8, 2003.

———. 1992d. SNC Allows Political Parties, Free Press; Prisoners to be Freed. *Agence France Presse*, January 14, 1992. Available from Lexis-Nexis, http://www.lexisnexis.com. Accessed July 8, 2003.

————. 1996. Govt Suspends All Political Parties Not Represented in
Parliament. *Agence France Presse*, May 1, 1996. Available from Lexis-
Nexis, http://www.lexisnexis.com. Accessed July 8, 2003.

————. 1997. Malaysia Sees Need to Avoid 'Hasty Decision' on Cambodian
Aid. 1997. *Agence France Presse*, July 21, 1997. Available from Lexis-
Nexis, http://www.lexisnexis.com. Accessed July 8, 2003.

Akashi, Yasushi. 1994. The Challenge of Peacekeeping in Cambodia.
International Peacekeeping 1 (2):204-215.

Americas Watch. 1993. Accountability and Human Rights: The Report of the
United Nations Commission on the Truth for El Salvador. New York and
Washington: Americas Watch.

Anstee, Margaret. 1995. Book Reviews. *Journal of Southern African Studies* 21
(2):335-338. Available from EBSCO Host, http://web13/epnet.com.
Accessed March 18, 2003.

Anstee, Margaret Joan. 1996. *Orphan of the Cold War: The Inside Story of the
Collapse of the Angolan Peace Process, 1992-93*. New York: St. Martin's
Press.

Asiaweek. 1994. A Purge in Phnom Penh; Did The Finance Minister Ask Too
Many Questions? *Asiaweek*, p. 36. Available from Lexis-Nexis,
http://www.lexisnexis.com. Accessed July 8, 2003.

Babb, Joseph G. D., and George W. Steuber. 1998. UN Operations in
Cambodia: (A Second "Decent Interval"). In *"The Savage Wars of Peace"*:
Toward a New Paradigm of Peace Operations, edited by J. T. Fishel.
Boulder: Westview Press.

Baloyra, Enrique A. 1998. El Salvador: From Reactionary Despotism to
Partidocracia. In *Postconflict Elections, Democratization, and
International Assistance*, edited by K. Kumar. Boulder: Lynne Rienner.

Baranyi, Stephen, and Liisa North. 1992. Stretching the Limits of the Possible:
United Nations Peacekeeping in Central America. Ottawa: Canadian Centre
for Global Security.

Baranyi, Stephen, and Liisa L. North. 1996. The United Nations in El Salvador:
The Promise and Dilemmas of an Integrated Approach to Peace. Ontario:
Centre for Research on Latin America and the Caribbean, York University.

Barnett, Michael N. 1999. Peacekeeping, Indifference, and Genocide in
Rwanda. In *Cultures of Insecurity: States, Communities and the Production
of Danger*, edited by J. Weldes, M. Laffey, H. Gusterson and R. Duvall.
Minneapolis: University of Minnesota Press.

Bar-Simon-Tov. 1994. *Israel and the Peace Process, 1977-1982: In Search of
Legitimacy for Peace*. Edited by R. Stone, *SUNY Series in Israeli Studies*.
Albany, NY: State University of New York Press.

Bercovitch, Jacob, and Allison Houston. 1996. The Study of International
Mediation: Theoretical Issues and Empirical Evidence. In *Resolving
International Conflicts: The Theory and Practice of Mediation*, edited by J.
Bercovitch. Boulder: Lynne Rienner.

Berdal, Mats R. 1993. *Whither UN Peacekeeping?* Adelphi Paper 281. London: International Institute for Strategic Studies.

Bertram, Eva. 1995. Reinventing Government: The Promise and Perils of United Nations Peace Building. *Journal of Conflict Resolution* 39 (3):387-418.

Birgisson, Karl. 1993. United Nations Special Committee on the Balkans. In *The Evolution of UN Peacekeeping: Case Studies and Comparative Analysis*, edited by W. J. Durch. New York: St. Martin's Press.

Birsel, Robert. 1991. Cambodian Factions in Hard Bargaining Ahead of Meetings With World Power. *Agence France Presse*, August 28, 1991. Available from Lexis-Nexis, http://www.lexisnexis.com. Accessed July 8, 2003.

Bosch, Brian J. 1999. *The Salvadoran Officer Corps and the Final Offensive of 1981*. Jefferson, NC: McFarland and Company, Inc.

Boutros-Ghali, Boutros. 1995a. Introduction. In *The United Nations and El Salvador 1990-1005*. New York: United Nations Department of Public Information.

———. 1995b. Introduction. In *The United Nations and Cambodia, 1991-1995*. New York, New York: United Nations Department of Public Information.

Boyce, James K. 1995. External Assistance and the Peace Process in El Salvador. *World Development* 23 (12):2101-2116.

———. 2002. *Investing in Peace: Aid and Conditionality After Civil Wars*. Adelphi Paper #351. Oxford/New York: Oxford University Press for The International Institute for Strategic Studies.

Boyce, James K., and Manuel Pastor, Jr. 1998. 'Aid for Peace: Can International Financial Institutions Help Prevent Conflict?' World Policy Journal 15 (2): 42–49.

Bratt, Duane. 1997. Assessing the Success of UN Peacekeeping Operations. In *The UN, Peace and Force*, edited by M. Pugh. London: Frank Cass.

British Broadcasting Corporation. 1995a. President Calderon Sol Reaffirms Commitment to Consolidation of Peace. In *BBC Summary of World Broadcasts*. Original edition, San Salvador Radio and TV Stations 1 June 1995. Available from Lexis-Nexis, http://www.lexisnexis.com. Accessed June 13, 2003.

———. 1995b. Hun Sen Accuses USA, Other Foreign Countries, of Interfering in Cambodian Affairs. *BBC Summary of World Broadcasts*, Original edition, National Voice of Cambodia, 4 December 1995. Available from Lexis-Nexis, http://www.lexisnexis.com. Accessed July 8, 2003.

———. 1995c. First Prime Minister Ranariddh Warns Western Countries Not to Interfere in Internal. *BBC Summary of World Broadcasts*. Original edition Reaksmei Kampuchea (Phnom Penh, Cambodia) December 9, 1995, p. 12 Available from Lexis-Nexis, http://www.lexisnexis.com. Accessed July 8, 2003.

———. 1996. Second Premier Welcomes US Congressional Approval of Most-Favoured-Nation Status. *BBC Summary of World Broadcasts*. Original edition National Voice of Cambodia, 27 July 1996. Available from Lexis-Nexis, http://www.lexisnexis.com. Accessed July 8, 2003.

———. 1997. Malaysian Foreign Minister Says ASEAN in No Hurry to Suspend Aid to Cambodia. *BBC Summary of World Broadcasts*, Original edition TV3 Televisions (Kuala Lampur) July 21, 1997. Available from Lexis-Nexis, http://www.lexisnexis.com. Accessed July 8, 2003.

Brown, Frederick Z. 1998. Cambodia's Rocky Venture in Democracy. In *Postconflict Elections, Democratization, and International Assistance*, edited by K. Kumar. Boulder: Lynne Rienner.

Brown, MacAlister, and Joseph J. Zasloff. 1998. *Cambodia Confounds the Peacemakers, 1979 - 1998*. Ithaca: Cornell University Press.

Burton, John. 1990. *Conflict: Resolution and Provention*. New York: St. Martin's Press.

Byrne, Hugh. 1996. *El Salvador's Civil War: A Study of Revolution*. Boulder: Lynne Rienner.

Calderon Sol, Armando. 2003. *Inaugural Address* (BBC Summary of World Broadcasts). British Broadcasting Corporation. Available from Lexis-Nexis, http://www.lexisnexis.com. Accessed June 16, 2003.

Chanda, Nayan. 1990. Japan's Quiet Entrance on the Diplomatic Stage. *Christian Science Monitor*, June 13, 1990. Available from Lexis-Nexis, http://www.lexisnexis.com. Accessed July 8, 2003.

Cousens, Elizabèth M. 2001. Introduction. In *Peacebuilding as Politics: Cultivating Peace in Fragile Societies*, edited by E. M. Cousens and C. K. W. K. Wemester. Boulder: Lynne Rienner.

Cristiani, Alfredo. 1993. Documents on Democracy. *Journal of Democracy* 4 (2):138-139.

Crocker, Chester A. 1996. The Varieties of Intervention: Conditions for Success. In *Managing Global Chaos: Sources of and Responses to International Conflict*, edited by C. A. Crocker and F. O. Hampson. Washington, D. C.: United States Institute of Peace Press.

Curtis, Grant. 1998. *Cambodia Reborn? The Transition to Democracy and Development*. Washington, D.C. and Geneva: Brookings Institution Press and The United Nations Research Institute for Social Development.

Dahl, Robert A. 1989. *Democracy and Its Critics*. New Haven: Yale UP.

Dalton, Juan Jose. 2003. *El Salvador: Military No Longer Above the Law*. Inter Press Service. July 1, 1994. Available from Lexis-Nexis, http://www.lexisnexis.com. Accessed June 16, 2003.

Darling, Juanita. 1997. *Politics: Divided El Salvador Congress Finds Room for Cooperation*. Los Angeles Times. J. July 4, 1997, A4. Available from Lexis-Nexis, http://www.lexisnexis.com. Accessed March 13, 2000.

David, Steven R. 1997. Internal War: Causes and Cures. *World Politics* 49 (4):52-76.

Davidson, Ian. 1990. Cambodian peace talks make progress. *Financial Times*, December 24, 1990, 3. Available from Lexis-Nexis, http://www.lexisnexis.com. Accessed July 8, 2003.

de Soto, Alvaro. 1999. Ending Violent Conflict in El Salvador. In *Herding Cats: Multiparty Mediation in a Complex World*, edited by C. A. Crocker, F. O. Hampson and P. Aall. Washington, D.C.: United States Institute of Peace Press.

del Castillo, Graciana. 1997. The arms-for-land deal in El Salvador. In *Keeping the Peace: Multidimensional UN Operations in Cambodia and El Salvador*, edited by M. W. Doyle, I. Johnstone and R. C. Orr. Cambridge: Cambridge University Press.

Diamond, Larry. 1996. Democracy in Latin America: Degrees, Illusions, and Directions for Consolidation. In *Beyond Sovereignty: Collectively Defending Democracy in the Americas*, edited by T. Farer. Baltimore and London: The Johns Hopkins University Press.

Diamond, Larry, Marc F. Plattner, Yun-han Chu, and Hung-mao Tien, eds. 1997. *Consolidating the Third Wave Democracies: Regional Challenges*. Vol. 2. Baltimore, MD: The Johns Hopkins University Press.

Diehl, Paul F. 1994. *International Peacekeeping*. Baltimore: The Johns Hopkins University Press. Original edition, 1993.

Donnelly, Jack. 2003. *Universal Human Rights in Theory and Practice*. 2nd ed. Ithaca and London: Cornell University Press. Original edition, 2003.

Doyle, Michael, and Nishkala Suntharanlingam. 1994. The UN in Cambodia: Lessons for Complex Peacekeeping. *International Peacekeeping* 1 (2):117-147.

Doyle, Michael W. 1994. UNTAC: Sources of Success and Failure. In *International Peacekeeping: Building on the Cambodian Experience*, edited by H. Smith. Canberra: Australian Defence Studies Centre.

———. 1995. *UN Peacekeeping in Cambodia: UNTAC's Civil Mandate*, *International Peace Academy Occasional Paper Series*. Boulder and London: Lynne Rienner.

———. 2001. Peacebuilding in Cambodia: Legitimacy and Power. In *Peacebuilding as Politics: Cultivating Peace in Fragile Societies*, edited by E. M. Cousens and C. Kumar. Boulder: Lynne Rienner.

Doyle, Michael W. , and Ayaka Suzuki. 1995. Transitional Authority in Cambodia. In *The United Nations and Civil Wars*, edited by T. G. Weiss. Boulder and London: Lynne Rienner.

Doyle, Michael W., Ian Johnstone, and Robert C. Orr, eds. 1997. *Keeping the Peace: Multidimensional UN Operations in Cambodia and El Salvador*. Cambridge: Cambridge University Press.

Duarte, José Napoleón. 1990. Inaugural Address (1984). In *The Human Rights Reader*, edited by W. Laqueur and B. Rubin. New York: Meridian.

Durch, William J. 1996. Keeping the Peace: Politics and Lessons of the 1990s. In *UN Peacekeeping, American Politics, and the Uncivil Wars of the 1990s*, edited by W. J. Durch. New York: St. Martin's Press.

———, ed. 1993. *The Evolution of UN Peacekeeping: Case Studies and Comparative Analysis*. New York: St. Martin's Press.

Durch, William J., and James A. Schear. 1996. Faultlines: UN Operations in the Former Yugoslavia. In *UN Peacekeeping, American Politics, and the Uncivil Wars of the 1990s*, edited by W. A. Durch. New York: St. Martin's Press.

Evans, Gareth. 1994. The Comprehensive Political Settlement to the Cambodia Conflict: An Exercise in Cooperation for Peace. In *International Peacekeeping: Building on the Cambodian Experience*, edited by H. Smith. Canberra: Australian Defence Studies Centre.

Farer, Tom. 1996. Collectively Defending Democracy in the Western Hemisphere. In *Beyond Sovereignty: Collectively Defending Democracy in the Americas*, edited by T. Farer. Baltimore and London: The Johns Hopkins University Press.

Financial Times. 1991. Cambodian Factions Agree Arms Curbs; UN Peace Plan Makes Slow Progress. *Financial Times*, June 25, 1991, 14. Available from Lexis-Nexis, http://www.lexisnexis.com. Accessed July 8, 2003.

Findlay, Trevor. 1995. Cambodia: The Legacy and Lessons of UNTAC. Oxford: SIPRI.

Finnemore, Martha, and Kathryn Sikkink. 1998. International Norm Dynamics and Political Change. *International Organization* 52 (4):887-917.

Fishel, John T. 1998. War By Other Means? The Paradigm and its Application to Peace Operations. In *"The Savage Wars of Peace": Toward a New Paradigm of Peace Operations*, edited by J. T. Fishel. Boulder: Westview Press.

Forsythe, David P. 1996. The United Nations, Democracy and the Americas. In *Beyond Sovereignty: Collectively Defending Democracy in the Americas*, edited by T. Farer. Baltimore and London: The Johns Hopkins University Press.

Fortna, Virginia Page. 1995. Success and Failure in Southern Africa: Peacekeeping in Namibia and Angola. In *Beyond Traditional Peacekeeping*, edited by D. C. F. Daniel and B. C. Hayes. New York: St. Martin's Press.

Gottesman, Evan R. 2003. *Cambodia after the Khmer Rouge: Inside the Politics of Nation Building*. New Haven & London: Yale University Press.

Goulding, Marrack. 1993. The Evolution of United Nations Peacekeeping. *International Affairs* 69 (3):451-464.

Gray, Denis D. 1996. Power Struggles, Violence, Threaten Cambodian Democracy. *The Associated Press*, June 17, 1996. Available from Lexis-Nexis, http://www.lexisnexis.com. Accessed July 8, 2003.

Gruson, Lindsey. 1989a. Likely Rightist Victory in El Salvador Poses Major Policy Challenge for U.S. *The New York Times*, March 19, 1989, A3. Available from Lexis-Nexis, http://www.lexisnexis.com. Accessed April 18, 2003.

————. 1989b. Newcomer Sworn as Salvador's Leader. *The New York Times*, June 2, 1989, A3. Available from Lexis-Nexis, http://www.lexisnexis.com. Accessed April 18, 2003.

Hampson, Fen Osler. 1996a. *Nurturing Peace: Why Peace Settlements Succeed or Fail.* Washington, D.C.: United States Institute of Peace Press.
———. 1996b. The Pursuit of Human Rights: The United Nations in El Salvador. In *UN Peacekeeping, American Politics and the Uncivil Wars of the 1990s,* edited by W. J. Durch. New York: St. Martin's Press.
———. 1996c. Why Orphaned Peace Settlements Are More Prone to Failure. In *Managing Global Chaos: Sources of and Responses to International Conflict,* edited by C. A. Crocker and F. O. Hampson. Washington, D.C.: United States Institute of Peace Press.
Handal, Jorge Shafik. 1993. Documents on Democracy. *Journal of Democracy* 4 (2):138-139.
Hansen, Annika S. 1997. Political Legitimacy, Confidence-building and the Dayton Peace Agreement. *International Peacekeeping* 4 (2):74-90.
Haq, Farhan. 1997. Cambodia-Rights: U.N. Tries to Aid Return of Political Exiles. *Inter Press Service,* November 27, 1997. Available from Lexis-Nexis, http://www.lexisnexis.com. Accessed July 8, 2003.
Heininger, Janet E. 1994. *Peacekeeping in Transition: The United Nations in Cambodia.* New York: The Twentieth Century Fund Press.
Higgins, Rosalyn. 1969. *United Nations Peacekeeping 1946-1967 Documents and Commentary.* Vol. 1. London: Royal Institute of International Affairs: Oxford University Press.
———. 1981. *United Nations Peacekeeping: Documents and Commentary.* Vol. IV. Oxford: Oxford University Press.
Hill, Stephen M., and Shanin P. Malik. 1996. *Peacekeeping and the United Nations.* Edited by S. Croft, *Security Studies Research Programme.* Aldershot: Dartmouth Publishing Company Limited.
Holiday, David, and William Stanley. 1993. Building the Peace: Preliminary Lessons from El Salvador. *Journal of International Affairs* 46 (2):415-438.
Horowitz. 1985. *Ethnic Groups in Conflict.* Berkeley: University of California Press.
Huntington, Samuel P. 1991. *The Third Wave: Democratization in the Late Twentieth Century.* Norman and London: University of Oklahoma Press.
Hurd, Ian. 1999. Legitimacy and Authority in International Politics. *International Organization* 53 (2):379-408.
Jablonsky, David, and James S. McCallum. 1999. Peace Implementation and the Concept of Induced Consent in Peace Operations. *Parameters* 29 (1):54-70. Available from Lexis-Nexis, http://www.lexisnexis.com. Accessed March 20, 2001.
James, Alan. 1990. *Peacekeeping in International Politics.* New York: St. Martin's Press.
———. 1992a. Internal Peacekeeping. Paper read at Peacekeeping and the Challenge of Civil Conflict Resolution: Proceedings of the Sixth Annual Conflict Studies Conference, September 1992, at University of New Brunswick.

116 *Bibliography*

————. 1993. The History of Peacekeeping: An Analytical Perspective. *Canadian Defense Quarterly* 23 (1):10. Available from Proquest, http://www.proquest.umi.com. Accessed March 20, 2001.

James, W. Martin. 1992b. *A Political History of the Civil War in Angola 1974-1990*. New Brunswick, NJ: Transaction Publishers.

Jeldres, Julio A. 1993. The UN and the Cambodian Transition. *Journal of Democracy* 4 (4):104-116.

Jett, Dennis C. 1999. *Why Peacekeeping Fails*. New York: St. Martin's Press.

Johnstone, Ian. 1995. *Rights and Reconciliation: UN Strategies in El Salvador*. Boulder and London: Lynne Rienner.

————. 1997. Rights and Reconciliation in El Salvador. In *Keeping the Peace: Multidimensional UN Operations in Cambodia and El Salvador*, edited by M. W. Doyle, I. Johnstone and R. C. Orr. Cambridge: Cambridge University Press.

Jordens, Jay. 1996. Persecution of Cambodia's Ethnic Vietnamese Communities During and Since the UNTAC Period. In *Propaganda, Politics, and Violence in Cambodia: Democratic Transition under United Nations Peace-keeping*, edited by S. Heder and J. Ledgerwood. Armonk, New York: M. E. Sharpe.

Joyner, Christopher C. 1999. The United Nations and Democracy. *Global Governance* 5 (3):333-357.

Juhn, Tricia. 1998. *Negotiating Peace in El Salvador: Civil-Military Relations and the Conspiracy to End the War*. New York: St. Martin's Press.

Kagan, Donald. 1995. *On the Origins of War and the Preservation of Peace*. New York: Anchor Books.

Kamm, Henry. 1994. Despite U.N.'s Effort, Cambodia is Chaotic. *The New York Times*, July 4, 1994, A1. Available from Lexis-Nexis, http://www.lexisnexis.com. Accessed July 8, 2003.

————. 1998. *Cambodia: Report from a Stricken Land*. New York: Arcade Publishing.

Karl, Terry Lynn. 1992. El Salvador's Negotiated Revolution. *Foreign Affairs* 71 (2):147-164.

Kellas, John G. 1991. *The Politics of Nationalism and Ethnicity*. New York: St. Martin's Press.

Kiernan, Ben, ed. 1993. *Genocide and Democracy in Cambodia: The Khmer Rouge, the United Nations and the International Community*. New Haven: Yale University Press.

King, Charles. 1997. *Ending Civil Wars*. New York and Oxford: Oxford University Press.

Knudsen, Christine M, with I. William Zartman. 1995. The Large Small War in Angola. *The Annals of the American Academy of Political and Social Science* 541 (September):130-143.

Kovaleski, Serge F. 1999. Pessimistic Salvadorans Prepare to Vote. *The Washington Post*, March 7, 1999, A21. Available from Lexis-Nexis, http://www.lexisnexis.com. Accessed June 1, 1999.

Kumar, Chetan. 2001. Conclusion. In *Peacebuilding as Politics: Cultivating Peace in Fragile Societies*, edited by E. M. Cousens and W. K. W. Chetan Kumar. Boulder: Lynne Rienner.

Kumar, Krishna. 1998. Postconflict Elections and International Assistance. In *Postconflict Elections, Democratization, and International Assistance*, edited by K. Kumar. Boulder: Lynne Rienner.

Lankevich, George J. 2001. *The United Nations under Javier Perez de Cuellar, 1982 - 1991*. Lanham, Maryland and London: The Scarecrow Press, Inc.

Lederach, John Paul. 1997. *Building Peace: Sustainable Reconciliation in Divided Societies*. Washington, D.C.: United Stated Institute of Peace Press.

Ledgerwood, Judy. 1996. Patterns of CPP Political Repression and Violence During the UNTAC Period. In *Propaganda, Politics, and Violence in Cambodia: Democratic Transition Under United Nations Peace-keeping*, edited by S. Heder and J. Ledgerwood. Armonk, New York: M. E. Sharpe.

LeVine, Mark. 1997. Peacemaking in El Salvador. In *Keeping the Peace: Multidimensional UN Operations in Cambodia and El Salvador*, edited by M. W. Doyle, I. Johnstone and R. C. Orr. Cambridge: Cambridge University Press.

Licklider, Roy. 2001. Obstacles to Peace Settlement. In *Turbulent Peace: The Challenges of Managing International Conflict*, edited by C. A. Crocker, F. O. Hampson and P. Aall. Washington, DC: United States Institute of Peace Press.

————, ed. 1993. *Stopping the Killing: How Civil Wars End*. New York and London: New York University Press.

Linz, Juan J., and Alfred Stepan. 1996. *Problems of Democratic Transition and Consolidation: Southern Europe, South America, and Post-Communist Europe*. Baltimore: The Johns Hopkins University Press.

Linz, Juan, and Alfred Stepan. 1989. Political Crafting of Democratic Consolidation or Destruction: European and South American Comparisons. In *Democracy in the Americas: Stopping the Pendulum*, edited by R. A. Pastor. New York: Holmes & Meier.

Lizee, Pierre P. 1997. Cambodia in 1996: Of Tigers, Crocodiles, and Doves. *Asian Survey* 37 (1):65-71.

————. 2000. *Peace, Power and Resistance in Cambodia: Global Governance and the Failure of International Conflict Resolution*. New York: St. Martin's Press.

Lund, Michael S. 1996. Early Warning and Preventive Diplomacy. In *Managing Global Chaos: Sources of and Responses to International Conflict*, edited by C. A. Crocker and F. O. Hampson. Washington, D. C.: United States Institute of Peace Press.

Lungo Uclés, Mario. 1990. *El Salvador in the Eighties: Counterinsurgency and Revolution*. Translated by A. F. Shogan. Philadelphia: Temple University Press.

Mackinlay, John, and Jarat Chopra. 1992. Second Generation Multinational Operations. *Washington Quarterly* 15 (3):114. Available from Lexis-Nexis, http://www.lexisnexis.com. Accessed August 4, 2001.

MacQueen, Norrie. 1998. Peacekeeping by Attrition: The United Nations in Angola. *The Journal of Modern African Studies* 36 (3):399-422.

McCormick, David H. 1997. From Peacekeeping to Peacebuilding: Restructuring Military and Police Institutions in El Salvador. In *Keeping the Peace: Multidimensional UN operations in Cambodia and El Salvador*, edited by M. W. Doyle, I. Johnstone and R. C. Orr. Cambridge: Cambridge University Press.

McIlwaine, Cathy. 1998. Contesting Civil Society: Reflections from El Salvador. *Third World Quarterly* 19 (4):651-672.

McNamara, Dennis. 1995. UN Human Rights Activities in Cambodia: An Evaluation. In *Honoring Human Rights and Keeping the Peace: Lessons from El Salvador, Cambodia and Haiti*, edited by A. H. Henkin. Washington, D. C.: The Aspen Institute.

Miller, Linda B. 1967. *World Order and Local Disorder: The United Nations and Internal Conflicts.* Princeton, NJ: Princeton UP.

Miller, Marjorie. 1999. Salvadoran Revolutionary is a Compromiser in Exile. *Los Angeles Times*, March 6, 1999, A1. Available from Lexis-Nexis, http://www.lexisnexis.com. Accessed March 13, 2000.

Montgomery, Tommie Sue. 1995a. Getting to Peace in El Salvador: the Roles of the United Nations Secretariat and ONUSAL. *Journal of Interamerican Studies and World Affairs* 37 (4):139-172.

———. 1995b. *Revolution in El Salvador: From Civil Strife to Civil Peace.* 2nd ed. Boulder: Westview Press.

Munck, Gerardo L., and Chetan Kumar. 1995. Civil Conflicts and the Condition for Successful International Intervention: A Comparative Study of Cambodia and El Salvador. *Review of International Studies* 21 (2):159-181.

———. 1998. Conflict Resolution and International Intervention in El Salvador and Cambodia. In *Resolving Regional Conflicts*, edited by R. E. Kanet. Urbana: University of Illinois Press.

Neou, Kasie, and Jeffrey C. Gallup. 1999. Conducting Cambodia's Elections. *Journal of Democracy* 10 (2):152-164.

Neuberger, Benyamin. 1986. *National Self-Determination in Postcolonial Africa.* Boulder: Lynne Rienner.

Nordlinger, Eric A. 1972. *Conflict Regulation in Divided Societies.* Cambridge, MA: Center for International Affairs, Harvard University.

Ohlson, Thomas, and Stephen John Stedman. 1994. *The New is Not Yet Born: Conflict Resolution in Southern Africa.* Washington, D.C.: The Brookings Institution.

Ojendal, Joakim. 2001. Democracy Lost? The Fate of the U.N.-implanted Democracy in Cambodia. In *Cambodia: Change and Continuity in Contemporary Politics*, edited by S. Peau. Adlershot: Ashgate.

Omang, Joanne. 1983. U.S. Calls Nicaraguan Offer Deficient; Regional Solution to Central American Conflict Termed First Priority. *The Washington Post*, October 22, 1983, A11. Available from Lexis-Nexis, http://www.lexisnexis.com. Accessed March 7, 2003.

Orr, Robert C. 2001. Building Peace in El Salvador: From Exception to Rule. In *Peacebuilding as Politics: Cultivating Peace in Fragile Societies*, edited by E. M. Cousens and C. Kumar. Boulder, CO: Lynne Rienner Publishers.

O'Shaughnessy, Laura Nuzzi, and Michael Dodson. 1999. Political Bargaining and Democratic Transitions: A Comparison of Nicaragua and El Salvador. *Journal of Latin American Studies* 31 (1):99-127.

Ott, Marvin C. 1997. Cambodia: Between Hope and Despair. *Current History* 96 (614):431-436.

Ottaway, Marina. 1998. Angola's Failed Elections. In *Postconflict Elections, Democratization, and International Assistance*, edited by K. Kumar. Boulder: Lynne Rienner.

Parsons, Anthony. 1995. *From Cold War to Hot Peace: UN Interventions 1947-1994*. London: Michael Joseph.

Pearce, Jenny. 1999. Peace-building in the Periphery: Lessons from Central America. *Third World Quarterly* 20 (1):51-68.

Peceny, Mark. 1999. The Social Construction of Democracy. *International Studies Review* 1 (1):95-102.

Peou, Sorpong. 1998. Cambodia in 1997: Back to Square One? *Asian Survey* 38 (1):69-74.

———. 2000. *Intervention and Change in Cambodia: Towards Democracy?* New York and Singapore: St Martin's Press and the Institute of Southeast Asian Studies.

Pirnie, Bruce. 1994. A Typology for Peace Operations. *Military Science and Modeling* 6 (November 1994):21-23.

Prasad, M. Nagendra. 2001. *Indonesia's Role in the Resolution of the Cambodian Problem*. Aldershot: Ashgate.

Purcell, Susak Kaufman. 1985. Demystifying Contadora. *Foreign Affairs* 64 (1):74-95. Available from Lexis-Nexis, http://www.lexisnexis.com. Accessed May 15, 2003.

Ratner, Steven R. 1993a. The Cambodia Settlement Agreements. *American Journal of International Law* 87 (1):1-41.

———. 1993b. The United Nations in Cambodia: A Model for Resolution of Internal Conflicts? In *Enforcing Restraint: Collective Intervention in Internal Conflicts*, edited by L. F. Damrosch. New York: Council on Foreign Relations Press.

———. 1995. *The New UN Peacekeeping: Building Peace in Lands of Conflict After the Cold War*. New York: St. Martin's Press.

Richardson, Michael. 1997a. U.S. Seeks 'Tough' Cambodia Line. *International Herald Tribune*, July 19, 1997, 7. Available from Lexis-Nexis, http://www.lexisnexis.com. Accessed July 8, 2003.

————. 1997b. US envoy urges donors to use aid as democracy chip. *The Australian*, July 21, 1997, 6. Available from Lexis-Nexis, http://www.lexisnexis.com. Accessed July 8, 2003.

Roberts, David. 1998. Meddling While Phnom Penh Burned: The U.S. Role in the Cambodian Secession. *Bulletin of Concerned Asian Scholars* 30 (3):14-24.

Roberts, David W. 2001. *Political Transition in Cambodia 1991-1999: Power, Elitism and Democracy*. New York: St. Martin's Press.

Rothschild, Joseph. 1981. *Ethnopolitics: A Conceptual Framework*. New York: Columbia University Press.

Ruggie, John Gerard. 1983. International Regimes, Transactions and Change: Embedded Liberalism in the Postwar Economic Order. In *International Regimes*, edited by S. D. Krasner. Ithaca: Cornell University Press.

————. 1998. *Constructing the World Polity*. London and New York: Routledge.

Rupesinghe, Kumar with Sanam Naraghi Anderlini. 1998. *Civil Wars, Civil Peace: An Introduction to Conflict Resolution*. London: Pluto Press.

Sanderson, J. M. 1994. UNTAC: Successes and Failures. In *International Peacekeeping: Building on the Cambodian Experience*, edited by H. Smith. Canberra: Australian Defence Studies Centre.

Sanderson, John M., and Michael Maley. 1998. Elections and Liberal Democracy in Cambodia. *Australian Journal of International Affairs* 52 (3):241-253.

Sanger, David E. 1991. Factions Meeting in Phnom Penh Appeal to U.N. for Peacekeepers. *The New York Times*, December 31, 1991, A2. Available from Lexis-Nexis, http://www.lexisnexis.com. Accessed July 8, 2003.

Schear, James A. 1996. Riding the Tiger: The United Nations and Cambodia's Struggle for Peace. In *UN Peacekeeping, American Politics, and the Uncivil Wars of the 1990s*, edited by W. J. Durch. New York: St. Martin's Press.

Sciolino, Elaine. 1989. Rebel Plan Splits U.S. and Salvador. *The New York Times*, January 27, 1989, A3. Available from Lexis-Nexis, http://www.lexisnexis.com. Accessed April 18, 2003.

Seper, Chris. 1998. Fear Pervades Cambodia's Election Campaign; U.N., Watchdog Group Criticize Government in Wake of Killings, Other Violence. *The Washington Post*, July 16, 1998, A22. Available from Lexis-Nexis, http://www.lexisnexis.com. Accessed June 1, 1999.

Shawcross, William. 1998. Murders Cast Shadow Over Cambodia's Poll. *Sunday Telegraph*, July 26, 1998, 31. Available from Lexis-Nexis, http://www.lexisnexis.com. Accessed June 1, 1999.

Snyder, Jack, and Robert Jervis. 1999. Civil War and the Security Dilemma. In *Civil Wars, Insecurity, and Intervention*, edited by B. F. Walter and J. Snyder. New York: Columbia University Press.

Spence, J., and G. Vickers. 1994. *A Negotiated Revolution? A Two Year Progress Report on the Salvadoran Peace Accords*. Cambridge, MA: Hemisphere Initiatives.

Spence, Jack, George Vickers, and David Dye. 1995. The Salvadoran Peace Accords and Democratization: A Three Year Progress Report and Recommendations. Cambridge, MA: Hemisphere Initiatives.

Stanley, William, and David Holiday. 1997. Peace Mission Strategy and Domestic Actors: UN Mediation, Verification and Institution-building in El Salvador. *International Peacekeeping* 4 (2):22-49.

Stedman, Stephen John. 1990. *Peacemaking in Civil War: International Mediation in Zimbabwe, 1974 - 1980.* Boulder and London: Lynne Rienner.

———. 2001. International Implementation of Peace Agreements in Civil Wars: Findings from a Study of Sixteen Cases. In *Turbulent Peace: The Challenges of Managing International Conflict*, edited by C. A. Crocker, F. O. Hampson and P. Aall. Washington, DC: United States Institute of Peace Press.

Takeda, Yasuhiro. 1998. Japan's Role in the Cambodian Peace Process: Diplomacy, Manpower and Finance. *Asian Survey* 38 (6):553-568.

Torres-Rivas, Edelberto. 1997. Insurrection and Civil War in El Salvador. In *Keeping the Peace: Multidimensional UN Operations in Cambodia and El Salvador*, edited by M. W. Doyle, I. Johnstone and R. C. Orr. Cambridge: Cambridge University Press.

Touval, Saadia, and I. William Zartman. 1985. Conclusion: Mediation in Theory and Practice. In *International Mediation in Theory and Practice*, edited by S. Touval and I. W. Zartman. Boulder: Westview Press with the Foreign Policy Institute.

United Nations. 1990. *The Blue Helmets: A Review of United Nations Peace-keeping.* 2nd edition. New York: United Nations Department of Public Information.

———. 1995a. *The United Nations and El Salvador 1990-1995.* Vol. 14, *The United Nations Blue Books Series*. New York: United Nations Department of Public Information.

———. 1995b. *The United Nations and Cambodia 1991-1995.* Vol. 2, *The United Nations Blue Books Series*. New York: United Nations Department of Public Information.

———. 1996. *The Blue Helmets: A Review of United Nations Peace-keeping.* 3rd edition. New York: United Nations Department of Public Information.

United Press International. 1993. U.S. donates cars to Salvadoran police. *United Press International*, July 11, 1993. Available from Lexis-Nexis, http://www.lexisnexis.com. Accessed June 13, 2003.

Urquhart, Brian. 1972. *Hammarskjold.* New York: Alfred A. Knopf.

———. 1987. *A Life in Peace and War.* New York: Harper and Row.

Wagner, Robert Harrison. 1993. The Causes of Peace. In *Stopping the Killing: How Civil Wars End*, edited by R. Licklider. New York: New York University Press.

Walter, Barbara F. 1997. The Critical Barrier to Civil War Settlement. *International Organization* 51 (3):335-364.

————. 1999. Designing Transitions from Civil War. In *Civil Wars, Insecurity, and Intervention*, edited by B. F. Walter and J. Snyder. New York: Columbia University Press.

————. 2002. *Committing to Peace: The Successful Settlement of Civil Wars.* Princeton and Oxford: Princeton University Press.

Weiss, Thomas G. 1994. The United Nations and Civil Wars. *The Washington Quarterly* 17 (4):139-159.

Wendt, Alex. 1999. *Social Theory of International Politics.* Cambridge: Cambridge University Press.

Wilkins, Timothy A. 1997. The El Salvador Peace Accords: Using International and Domestic Law Norms to Build Peace. In *Keeping the Peace: Multidimensional UN operations in Cambodia and El Salvador*, edited by M. W. Doyle, I. Johnstone and R. C. Orr. Cambridge: Cambridge University Press.

Wilkinson, Tracy. 1993a. Salvadoran Military Assails U.N. Report. *Los Angeles Times*, March 25, 1993, A6. Available from Lexis-Nexis, http://www.lexisnexis.com. Accessed March 13, 2000.

————. 1993b. Salvadoran President Criticizes U.N. Report. *Los Angeles Times*, March 25, 1993, A6. Available from Lexis-Nexis, http://www.lexisnexis.com. Accessed March 13, 2000.

Williams, Philip J., and Knut Walter. 1997. *Militarization and Demilitarization in El Salvador's Transition to Democracy.* Edited by B. R. DeWalt, Pittsburgh PA: University of Pittsburgh Press.

Wood, Elisabeth Jean. 2000. *Forging Democracy From Below: Insurgent Transitions in South Africa and El Salvador.* Edited by M. Levi, Cambridge: Cambridge UP.

Zartman, I. William. 1993. The Unfinished Agenda: Negotiating Internal Conflicts. In *Stopping the Killing: How Civil Wars End*, edited by R. Licklider. New York and London: New York University Press.

————. 1995. Dynamics and Constraints in Negotiations in Internal Conflicts. In *Elusive Peace: Negotiating an End to Civil Wars*, edited by I. W. Zartman. Washington, D.C.: The Brookings Institution.

————, ed. 1997. *Governance as Conflict Management: Politics and Violence in West Africa.* Washington, D.C.: Brooking Institution Press.

Zartman, I. William, and Saadia Touval. 1996. International Mediation in the Post-Cold War Era. In *Managing Global Chaos: Sources of and Responses to International Conflict*, edited by C. A. Crocker and F. O. Hampson. Washington, D. C.: United States Institute Of Peace Press.

Zartman, William. 1985. *Ripe for Resolution.* Oxford: Oxford University Press.

Index

About the Author

Lisa A. Hall MacLeod received her Ph.D. from the Graduate School of International Studies, University of Denver. She is Assistant Professor of International Studies at Soka University of America where she teaches courses on the United Nations, international law, human rights and peace and conflict resolution. Her research interests include international conflict resolution, international organization and the role of norms in international relations theory.